W9-APY-969

NEW DIRECTIONS FOR TEACHING AND LEARNING

Robert J. Menges, *Northwestern University*
EDITOR-IN-CHIEF

Marilla D. Svinicki, *University of Texas, Austin*
ASSOCIATE EDITOR

Developing New and Junior Faculty

Mary Deane Sorcinelli
University of Massachusetts at Amherst

Ann E. Austin
Michigan State University

EDITORS

Number 50, Summer 1992

JOSSEY-BASS PUBLISHERS
San Francisco

DEVELOPING NEW AND JUNIOR FACULTY
Mary Deane Sorcinelli, Ann E. Austin (eds.)
New Directions for Teaching and Learning, no. 50
Robert J. Menges, Editor-in-Chief
Marilla D. Svinicki, Associate Editor

© 1992 by Jossey-Bass Inc., Publishers. All rights reserved.

No part of this issue may be reproduced in any form—except for a brief
quotation (not to exceed 500 words) in a review or professional work—
without permission in writing from the publishers.

Microfilm copies of issues and articles are available in 16mm and 35mm,
as well as microfiche in 105mm, through University Microfilms Inc., 300
North Zeeb Road, Ann Arbor, Michigan 48106.

LC 85-644763   ISSN 0271-0633   ISBN 1-55542-764-2

NEW DIRECTIONS FOR TEACHING AND LEARNING is part of The Jossey-Bass
Higher and Adult Education Series and is published quarterly by Jossey-
Bass Inc., Publishers, 350 Sansome Street, San Francisco, California 94104.
Second-class postage paid at San Francisco, California, and at additional
mailing offices. POSTMASTER: Send address changes to Jossey-Bass Inc.,
Publishers, 350 Sansome Street, San Francisco, California 94104.

SUBSCRIPTIONS for 1992 cost $45.00 for individuals and $60.00 for institutions, agencies, and libraries.

EDITORIAL CORRESPONDENCE should be sent to Robert J. Menges, Northwestern University, Center for the Teaching Professions, 2003 Sheridan
Road, Evanston, Illinois 60208-2610.

Cover photograph by Richard Blair/Color & Light © 1990.

 The paper used in this journal is acid-free and meets the strictest
guidelines in the United States for recycled paper (50 percent
recycled waste, including 10 percent post-consumer waste). Manu-
factured in the United States of America.

CONTENTS

EDITORS' NOTES

Evidence is increasing that new and junior faculty find the initial years in academe to be a time of great stress as well as satisfaction. On the one hand, new and junior faculty enjoy flexibility in how they do their work, opportunities to learn and grow, and pleasures from interacting with students and engaging in their scholarly work. On the other hand, they often are frustrated by insufficient time to fulfill all demands, difficulty in establishing supportive collegial relationships, insufficient resources, fear of non-reappointment, and struggles in balancing work and personal life. The ability of junior faculty to meet the challenges of these early years is critical to their success in and satisfaction with an academic career.

Research also suggests that new and junior faculty need assistance on several fronts and that colleagues and administrators need to better understand how junior faculty develop careers and cope with career pressures. In fact, the willingness of institutions to learn about and provide support during the early years may be vital to their ability to attract and retain potential faculty members. Although faculty developers and administrators have tried various ways to respond to the needs of new faculty, until now a practical compendium of advice on how to foster the career development of new and junior faculty was not available. This volume, *Developing New and Junior Faculty,* attempts to remedy that omission.

The volume contains a variety of material written from different perspectives. It is organized around three main themes: (1) research findings concerning new and junior faculty, (2) model programs and strategies to support faculty development, and (3) organizational factors that affect both the success of the strategies and the experiences of new and junior faculty. In Chapter One, Martin J. Finkelstein and Mark W. LaCelle-Peterson review who the new and junior faculty are and highlight research findings on the work and career experiences of these faculty members. In Chapter Two, Deborah Olsen and Mary Deane Sorcinelli sketch a longitudinal portrait of the experiences, needs, and perceptions of new faculty, finding dramatic changes over time. Then, in Chapter Three, Mary Deane Sorcinelli presents current research on the causes of stress among new and junior faculty and suggests strategies that individuals can use to counter it.

With the case made that new and junior faculty have special concerns and needs, the direction of the volume turns in the fourth and subsequent chapters to descriptions of successful strategies and programs to support the newest members of the professoriate. In Chapter Four, L. Dee Fink writes from the perspective of a practitioner, offering sound advice on the development of orientation programs for new faculty. In Chapter Five, Robert Boice provides concrete ideas for increasing the effectiveness of mentors to new faculty. Chapters Six and Seven address ways to help junior faculty become established successfully in two of their primary areas of responsibility. In Chapter Six, Donald K. Jarvis looks at ways to improve junior faculty scholarship, examining strategies for the development of programs that really work. Then, in Chapter Seven, Ann E. Austin describes a teaching fellows program that helps junior faculty both improve their teaching and deal with other challenges. In conjunction with Chapter Eight, Austin also emphasizes the third theme of this volume: the organizational context in which new and junior faculty work. She identifies several organizational factors that affect the success of faculty development strategies such as teaching fellows programs. One critical ingredient in the organizational context is the role played by department chairs. In Chapter Eight, Daniel W. Wheeler offers a perspective on the department chair as a developer of faculty, identifying roles and support mechanisms that can be of value. The department chair can be the critical link in regard to whether new and junior faculty are aware of and choose to utilize the kinds of resources and programs advocated in this book. Finally, we close the volume with a summary of the challenges facing new and junior faculty. We also highlight the strategies recommended in this volume and encourage institutional leaders to take seriously their critical role in supporting junior colleagues.

This volume promises benefits to several different but overlapping audiences: faculty developers, administrators, students in the field of higher education, and new and junior faculty themselves. The book brings together a wide range of fresh ideas and possibilities for the development of new and junior faculty. Armed with such information, faculty developers will be in a particularly advantageous position to set out initiatives and new programs in order to create more supportive and stimulating environments for the newest members of their academic communities. The volume also can assist department chairs, deans, and other administrators in their efforts to support and encourage the vitality of a critical institutional resource, the faculty. Finally, the volume raises questions and offers ideas that can help junior faculty who are experiencing the challenges described here, graduate students who are contemplating academic careers, and students of higher education.

Put simply, the volume provides a fresh slant on a difficult problem, offering new solutions and advice. Based on research findings concerning the characteristics and experiences of new and junior faculty, the contributors here describe the actions that individuals and institutions need to take in order to shape a positive beginning for these newcomers and to increase the likelihood that they will enjoy long and successful careers in academe. Demographers inform us that American higher education is moving into a period in which retirements will necessitate the hiring of many new faculty members. Thoughtful attention to their initial years in the academy will bring long-term benefits to not only the faculty members but also their students, colleagues, and institutions.

Mary Deane Sorcinelli
Ann E. Austin
Editors

MARY DEANE SORCINELLI is director of the Center for Teaching and associate adjunct professor in the Division of Educational Policy and Administration, University of Massachusetts, Amherst.

ANN E. AUSTIN is associate professor in the Department of Educational Administration at Michigan State University, East Lansing.

This chapter reviews who the new and junior faculty are and what the literature tells us about their experiences and careers.

New and Junior Faculty: A Review of the Literature

Martin J. Finkelstein, Mark W. LaCelle-Peterson

The attention that social scientists focus on a given social group tends to vary directly with its size or its status: The larger the group or the higher its status, the more attention it commands, and vice versa. The higher education literature on new and junior faculty confirms this generalization—with a vengeance. Until the pioneering but highly circumscribed work of Fink (1984) on ninety-seven new geography faculty, the literature was virtually silent on the subgroup. Since that time, the level of attention to new and junior faculty has been rising, although it cannot yet be considered genuinely high. What heightened interest there is proceeds, of course, from the new demographic realities of the academic profession in the United States: As a large segment of the profession hired in response to the explosive growth of the late 1960s and early 1970s prepares to retire in the late 1990s, new junior faculty will be needed in near record numbers to replace them. In addition, demographers anticipate that at the same time as this turnover takes place, enrollments will start to increase, heightening the need for new faculty members.

Currently, there is no "critical mass" of junior faculty ready to step into the shoes of their senior colleagues. As a result of the steady state in American higher education over the past two decades—low growth, except in a few fields (for example, business, computer science, and health science), and the concomitantly depressed academic job market—there has been limited hiring of new faculty. Moreover, many are anticipating a shortage of *potential* new and junior faculty in the pipeline (Bowen and Schuster, 1986; Bowen and Sosa, 1989) as a result of the stable number of Ph.D.'s produced by American graduate schools in the 1980s (especially in certain critical fields) and the declining popularity of academic careers among these Ph.D.'s (let alone as the occupational aspiration of current undergraduates). Thus, the recruitment and retention of this newly emergent group is now stimulating the interest of educational leaders, on the campus as well as in the state house.

In light of these developments and this interest, this chapter seeks (1) to identify and describe the major sources available to those who wish to learn about new and junior faculty and (2) to summarize what we have learned about this group that is relevant to those who shape their careers and depend on their optimal performance.

Data Sources on New and Junior Faculty

What we know about new and junior faculty comes from at least three basic sources: national surveys of higher education, general empirical studies of the American professoriate, and special empirical investigations of this emergent group.

National Surveys. Two kinds of national surveys provide relevant information about new and junior faculty. First, the annual survey of new doctoral recipients conducted by the National Research Council provides data on academic discipline, gender, ethnicity, current job prospects, and career plans of new Ph.D.'s, who constitute the major source of faculty for four-year colleges and universities. Comparative data have been available since the late 1960s. A ten-year summary of that data (National Research Council, 1986) showed that in virtually all fields, the proportion of doctoral recipients opting for careers in academe declined from the mid 1970s to the mid 1980s while the proportion opting for positions in industry increased (engineers were the sole stable group; just over one-quarter of recipients of doctorates in engineering consistently took positions in academe). These trends held for all groups, including women and minorities.

Second, recent national faculty surveys conducted by the National Center for Education Statistics (1989), the Carnegie Foundation for the Advancement of Teaching (1989), and the Higher Education Research Institute at the University of California, Los Angeles (Astin, Korn, and Dey, 1991) provide data on a nationally representative sample of faculty, typically disaggregated by age, rank, and/or tenure status. Many of the questions asked in these surveys parallel those asked on earlier national surveys, beginning in 1969 with the American Council on Education/Carnegie Council Survey (Bayer, 1973). These survey data provide a useful basis for comparing the current cohorts of junior faculty with past cohorts.

General Empirical Studies of the Professoriate. These include comprehensive national studies of the American professoriate as exemplified in Bowen and Schuster (1986) and Clark (1987). Also included in this group are more focused studies such as Burke's (1988) replication of the classic Caplow and McGee (1958) study of the hiring process and Baldwin and Blackburn's (1981) application of developmental theory to academic careers (see also Baldwin, 1990).

Special Studies of New and Junior Faculty. Over the past few years, a number of studies have focused explicitly on new and junior faculty. Some of these focus on career-related issues such as types of appointments (Blackburn and Wylie, 1985), time to tenure (Muller, 1986), and the balancing of work and personal life (Sorcinelli and Near, 1989). Others focus on the work experience, morale, and job satisfaction of new and junior faculty (Fink, 1984; Turner and Boice, 1987; Sorcinelli, 1988; Boice, 1991; Whitt, 1991). Most of this research involves either single-discipline studies that consider the experiences of new faculty in one discipline (for example, geography) at a number of institutions or single-institution studies that examine faculty from a number of departments in a single (almost always a large doctorate-granting) university. Only one study explicitly compares new and junior faculty with more experienced faculty who are also newcomers (Boice, 1991). In addition to these studies, Eimers's (1990) review of the background and experiences of new faculty and Fink's (1990) annotated review are helpful.

Taken together, these three basic sources illuminate three sets of questions: (1) Who are the new and junior faculty? (2) What are their careers like? And (3) what is the nature of their work experience?

Who Are the New and Junior Faculty?

Before addressing these three questions in relation to the current population, we need to consider the problem of delimiting the referent of the expression *new and junior faculty*. Unlike an original research study in which we can control selection of a sample from a defined population, we are faced here with a wide range of definitions across our various data sources. Among the national surveys, depending on the categories employed for data reporting, *junior faculty* (in most cases, the more inclusive group, of which new faculty (constitute a subgroup) are defined in fact by age (Carnegie Foundation for the Advancement of Teaching, 1989), rank and/or tenure status (the National Center for Education Statistics [1989] survey report includes faculty below the associate professor rank who are nontenured), and type of appointment (the Carnegie Foundation for the Advancement of Teaching [1989] survey includes only full-time faculty; and most surveys proportionately overrepresent tenure track, probationary appointees).

The most traditional definition of *new faculty* is those who have recently completed the Ph.D. or terminal professional degree and are ready to embark on a lifetime career in academe. While one of the most important studies in this area (Fink, 1984) involved ninety-seven new geography faculty who fit this bill, most of the recent studies (Turner and Boice, 1987; Sorcinelli, 1988; Boice, 1991; Whitt, 1991) have been institution-based and have thus included a broader range of faculty who are new to a particular institution (that is, people making a career change and faculty with experience in other institutions but new to the site of the study).

This diversity in definitions suggests that several distinct subgroups of new and junior faculty are treated and discussed across the literature. At this juncture, there is as yet insufficient subgroup-specific data to allow precise comparative intergroup analysis. Thus, we use the expression new and junior faculty somewhat loosely to refer to an imprecisely defined group of nontenured, full-time faculty below the rank of associate professor, including some who are new to the profession, some who are new to their current institution of employment, and some who are in the midst of probationary appointments (but clearly in contradistinction to experienced, tenured faculty in the senior ranks).

In light of these definitional ambiguities, what can we say about the character of the current crop of new and junior faculty? First, this group has chosen to "go against the trend." They have chosen to pursue academic work at a time when a decreasing proportion of Ph.D. recipients are making that choice; they have also managed to pursue and secure academic positions in a highly competitive "buyer's market." This success suggests that they are a highly purposeful and motivated group, less likely than earlier generations to reflect a modal pattern of casually "drifting into" academic careers for want of something better to do (Finkelstein, 1984; Gustad, 1960).

Second, compared to earlier generations, this cohort of new and junior faculty boasts a significantly higher proportion of women (33 to 50 percent among new hires at most types of institutions and in most nonscientific fields), which reflects the increasing proportional representation of women among Ph.D. recipients and among Ph.D. recipients choosing academic careers.

Third, today's new faculty entrants are an increasingly mature cohort. This increase in age reflects, in part, the longer average time periods taken to earn the Ph.D. and the pressures of an uncertain economy with declining support for graduate study (especially in the humanities and social sciences) and concomitant increases in part-time graduate study.

Fourth, this group is characterized by significant diversification in academic background. Overall, the last decade has witnessed a proliferation in the number of universities offering the Ph.D. degree (frequently combined with the downsizing of elite doctoral programs). This change, in turn, has led to two emergent developments: an increased diversification in the doctoral socialization experience of Ph.D. recipients trained at the "new" doctoral institutions (where programs often include more teaching and less research experience) and, owing to the tight marketplace, the employment of an increasing proportion of Ph.D. recipients from elite departments and institutions in less prestigious, regional, and even local four-year and two-year colleges (what Breneman and Youn [1988] have identified as the "trickle-down" effect). This latter development, especially, means that in one fashion or another increasing proportions of Ph.D.'s are encountering "culture shock" in their first appointments.

Finally, there is the matter of family situation. Reflecting general trends in the larger society, new faculty are more frequently than ever before part of dual-career couples, each of whom may be struggling independently with the juggling of career and personal matters. While no formal data are available, impressionistic evidence suggests a rise in dual-career couples as well as in commuter marriages among junior faculty (certainly vis-à-vis their senior colleagues).

Careers of New and Junior Faculty

What does the literature suggest about the career trajectory of this cohort of new and junior faculty? First, new and junior faculty increasingly find themselves in non-tenure track rather than probationary positions. While estimates vary by institutional type and field (higher at comprehensive and liberal arts colleges, lower at research universities; higher in foreign languages and humanities, generally), about one-third of new faculty appointments annually seem to fall into this category. There is some evidence that the number may be on the rise, or at least was on the rise during the 1980s; El-Khawas (1986) suggests just such a rise nationally. Blackburn and Wylie (1985) found no change in this category among a group of twelve liberal arts colleges during the 1980s, but nontenured or "term" appointments were already common at these institutions during the 1970s; untenured faculty at Great Lakes College Association member institutions in the 1980s were split nearly 50-50 between percentages of probationary and non-tenure track or term appointments. Moreover, a disproportionate share of these appointments were held by women. Women occupying these positions typically had been employed by fewer institutions for longer periods—they were, in short, less mobile (Muller, 1986; Blackburn and Wylie, 1985). While some of these non-tenure track faculty, especially women, may be constrained by geography from seeking opportunities, colleagues at the other extreme, known as academic nomads, appear to go from place to place in a series of temporary academic appointments (their numbers have not been precisely estimated; see Bowen and Schuster, 1986).

Those faculty who secure tenure track, probationary appointments are faced with many pressures, increasingly in the form of the imperative to publish in order to attain tenure (Bowen and Schuster, 1986). There is at least some evidence that at elite private universities those pressures are attenuated by the increasing practice of extending the probationary period (for example, from six years up to ten to twelve years at places such as Yale and Princeton; Sibley-Fries, 1986), which results in a whole other set of difficulties. Data on tenure rates do not clearly support the widely held perception that it is harder to get tenure now than it was a decade or two ago (Bowen and Schuster, 1986; Blackburn and Wylie, 1985). This fact may be a function of the increasing proportion of junior faculty who select themselves out prior to tenure review. As Blackburn and Wylie point out, even when institutional data on faculty is accessible, the task of determining in retrospect just why various individuals left an institution over a number of years is extremely difficult. While in the minds of junior faculty a negative tenure decision may be catastrophic and tantamount to career termination, at least at liberal arts colleges in the 1980s, most of those who were not awarded tenure were in fact able to move successfully to other academic positions (Blackburn and Wylie, 1985).

Work Experience of New and Junior Faculty

New and junior faculty work long and hard, at least forty-eight hours per week, in discharging their institutional responsibilities—a characteristic clearly comparable to the overall institutional commitments of their senior colleagues (National Center for Education Statistics, 1989). Moreover, the evidence from the university sector, at least, suggests that their work spills over into leisure pursuits and family life (Sorcinelli and Near, 1989) and becomes the central source of life satisfaction (Finkelstein, 1984).

If new and junior faculty work at least as much and as preemptively in their institutional role as do senior faculty, they nonetheless work *differently*. Junior faculty spend more time on teaching (especially non-tenure track faculty), are more involved in research leading in publication and in preparation of research grants, are less involved in institutional governance and administrative work (National Center for Education Statistics, 1989), and, overall, are more likely to experience severe time constraints (Carnegie Foundation for the Advancement of Teaching, 1989).

It is, then, not surprising that junior faculty (especially non-tenure track faculty) are generally less satisfied overall than are senior faculty. The sources of that dissatisfaction are, however, significant clues to the precise nature of the junior faculty work experience. New and junior faculty remain highly satisfied with their choice of an academic career and would, in percentages at least as high as senior colleagues (80 to 85 percent), choose it all over again. Where new and junior faculty are heartily disappointed is in their place within the employing institution. Barely one-half (versus nearly two-thirds of senior faculty; Carnegie Foundation for the Advancement of Teaching, 1989, p. 95) perceive their respective employing institutions as good places for them in the sense of providing opportunities for challenge and advancement. Indeed, the lack of collegiality (stimulating, supportive, and sustaining interaction with colleagues on professional issues), and the concomitant sense of isolation, emerges time and again as an overriding concern of new faculty and, to a slightly lesser extent, of more experienced junior faculty as well (Boice, 1991). Whatever degree of collegiality new faculty do experience involves their research and publication role rather than their teaching role, to which they devote the lion's share of their time and which remains the other central source of dissatisfaction.

Indeed, in pioneering work in the late 1970s, Fink (1984) found that new faculty were often overwhelmed by their teaching responsibilities. The time demands and uncertainties practically precluded reflection about teaching, though all participants in the study expressed a desire to teach well. Fully a decade later, Boice (1991) found no change for the better. At two universities—one a teaching-oriented university, the other a research university—he found that new faculty (in his study, new to the institution, whether experienced or inexperienced) tended to teach by lecturing, and that their concerns in teaching centered on getting the content right and avoiding bad student ratings, that is, they taught "defensively." New faculty, even those with prior teaching experience at other institutions, found teaching to be more demanding than expected and had little conception of how to improve their own performance. "New faculty," notes Boice (1991, p. 171), "establish comfort, efficiency, and student acceptance only slowly if at all." Boice found that new, inexperienced faculty members who were exemplary teachers (defined by their high student ratings, the researcher's classroom observations, and their own self-reports)—"quick starters," as he calls them—held positive attitudes toward students, lectured in a relaxed style that allowed for interaction with students, exhibited low levels of complaining about their campuses, actively sought advice about teaching from experienced colleagues, and quickly shifted their time commitments so that they spent relatively less time on teaching preparation than did their colleagues (less than 1.5 hours per classroom hour by their third semester) and relatively more time on scholarly and grant writing (on average, 3.3 hours per work week) (Boice, 1991, p. 168). He further reports that new faculty who were active in faculty development programs tended also to become more comfortable in the classroom and spent less time preparing lectures (most new faculty tend to overprepare for lectures) and more time on scholarly writing.

Boice's (1991) findings that new faculty are running hard just to keep in place, and feel unsupported in the undertaking, raise questions about the expectations and policies of the institutions that hired them, as well as questions about whether new faculty and their senior colleagues are on the same wavelength. Indeed, one study of new faculty and their administrators at a school of education suggests some of the dynamics at play. Whitt (1991) considered the experiences of six new faculty at the education school of a large midwestern research university (two of whom came straight from graduate school) and compared these new faculty members' experiences with school administrators' expectations and perceptions of those experiences. New faculty were disappointed in the level of collegiality experienced and found that they, rather than their senior colleagues, had to initiate interaction. Department chairs, while concerned about being supportive during new faculty members' adjustment to the school, clearly expected them to "hit the ground running." The high level of expectation was more clearly perceived by new faculty than was the intended level of support.

Discussion and Implications

Taken together, what do the research findings discussed here suggest about what we know and what we need to do? First, there appear to be some substantial commonalities in the careers and work experiences of new and junior faculty: similar degrees and sources of stress and similar needs for support. At the same time, there appear to be some substantial differences: The situation of non-tenure track faculty, for example, appears to differ in a number of respects from the situation of their probationary colleagues, the situation of women faculty (disproportionately represented among the non-tenure track group) differs from that of their male counterparts, and the situation of new faculty differs, especially in teaching-related matters, from that of their more experienced junior colleagues. It will behoove us in our future studies of this diverse group to take these differences as well as commonalities more explicitly into account for testing and elucidation.

Second, the research findings clearly document the need to support the work and budding careers of new and junior faculty. How that might best be done, and how it is already being accomplished during the early career years are the subjects of the other chapters in this volume.

While *post*appointment, *post*–career entry, on-the-job intervention is the most amenable target, it should be noted that the teaching-related concerns of new and junior faculty, in particular, harken us back as well to issues of preparation and of graduate education for academic careers. While over one-half of new faculty typically have some teaching assistant experience (Fink, 1984), the majority have not had total responsibility for a course. The role of graduate education in facilitating that transition is a critical issue that remains to be addressed. But that is a subject for another volume.

References

Astin, A. W., Korn, W., and Dey, E. *The American College Teacher: National Norms for the 1989–90 HERI Faculty Survey.* Los Angeles: Higher Education Research Institute, University of California, 1991.

Baldwin, R. G. "Faculty Career Stages and Implications for Professional Development." In J. H. Schuster, D. W. Wheeler, and Associates (eds.), *Enhancing Faculty Careers: Strategies for Development and Renewal.* San Francisco: Jossey-Bass, 1990.

Baldwin, R. G., and Blackburn, R. T. "The Academic Career as a Developmental Process: Implications for Higher Education." *Journal of Higher Education,* 1981, 52 (6), 598–614.

Bayer, A. E. *Teaching Faculty in Academe: 1972–73.* American Council on Education Research Reports, vol. 8, no. 2. Washington, D.C.: American Council on Education, 1973.

Blackburn, R., and Wylie, N. "Current Appointment and Tenure Practices: Their Impact on New Faculty Careers." Paper presented at the 9th annual meeting of the Association for the Study of Higher Education, Chicago, March 1985.

Boice, R. "New Faculty as Teachers." *Journal of Higher Education,* 1991, 62 (2), 150–173.

Bowen, H. R., and Schuster, J. H. *American Professors: A National Resource Imperiled.* New York: Oxford University Press, 1986.

Bowen, W., and Sosa, J. *Prospects for Faculty in the Arts and Sciences.* Princeton, N.J.: Princeton University Press, 1989.

Breneman, D., and Youn, T. *Academic Labor Market and Careers.* New York: Falmer Press, 1988.

Burke, D. *A New Academic Marketplace.* Westport, Conn.: Greenwood Press, 1988.

Caplow, T., and McGee, R. J. *The Academic Marketplace.* New York: Basic Books, 1958.

Carnegie Foundation for the Advancement of Teaching. *The Condition of the Professoriate: Attitudes and Trends, 1989.* Princeton, N.J.: Carnegie Foundation for the Advancement of Teaching, 1989.

Clark, B. *The Academic Life: Small Worlds, Different Worlds.* Princeton, N.J.: Carnegie Foundation for the Advancement of Teaching, 1987.

Eimers, M. "Background and Experiences of New Faculty." *Institutional Development,* 1990, 1 (3), 12–15.

El-Khawas, E. *Campus Trends, 1986.* Higher Education Panel Reports, no. 73. Washington, D.C.: American Council on Education, 1986.

Fink, L. D. (ed.). *The First Year of College Teaching.* New Directions for Teaching and Learning, no. 17. San Francisco: Jossey-Bass, 1984.

Fink, L. D. "New Faculty Members: The Professoriate of Tomorrow." *Journal of Staff, Program, and Organization Development,* 1990, 8 (4), 235–245.

Finkelstein, M. J. *The American Academic Profession.* Columbus: Ohio State University Press, 1984.

Gustad, J. *The Career Decisions of College Teachers.* Southern Regional Education Board Research Monographs, no. 2. Atlanta, Ga.: Southern Regional Education Board, 1960.

Muller, C. "Time to Tenure: The Intersection of Academic Careers and Family Patterns." Paper presented at the 67th annual meeting of the American Educational Research Association, San Francisco, April 1986.

National Center for Education Statistics. *Faculty in Higher Education Institutions, 1988.* Report of the 1988 National Survey of Postsecondary Faculty (NSOPF-88). Washington, D.C.: U.S. Department of Education, Office of Educational Research and Improvement, 1989.

National Research Council. *Summary Report, 1985: Doctorate Recipients from United States Universities.* Washington, D.C.: National Academy of Sciences, 1986.

Sibley-Fries, M. "Extended Probation at Research Universities." *Academe,* 1986, 72 (1), 37–40.

Sorcinelli, M. D. "Satisfactions and Concerns of New University Teachers." *To Improve the Academy,* 1988, 7, 121–131.

Sorcinelli, M. D., and Near, J. "Relations Between Work and Life Away from Work Among University Faculty." *Journal of Higher Education,* 1989, 60 (1), 59–81.

Turner, J. L., and Boice, R. "Starting at the Beginning: The Concerns and Needs of New Faculty." *To Improve the Academy,* 1987, 6, 41–55.

Whitt, E. J. " 'Hit the Ground Running': Experiences of New Faculty in a School of Education." *Review of Higher Education,* 1991, *14* (2), 177–197.

MARTIN J. FINKELSTEIN is director of the New Jersey Institute for Collegiate Teaching and Learning at Seton Hall University, South Orange.

MARK W. LACELLE-PETERSON is senior research associate at the New Jersey Institute for Collegiate Teaching and Learning.

This study finds evidence of dramatic shifts over time in pretenure faculty's views on teaching, research, tenure, and work satisfaction and stress.

The Pretenure Years:
A Longitudinal Perspective

Deborah Olsen, Mary Deane Sorcinelli

The early years of a faculty appointment are both difficult and critical to later academic success (Boice, 1991; Fink, 1984; Sorcinelli, 1988; Turner and Boice, 1987; Whitt, 1991). Yet, we know surprisingly little about the specific career tasks that pretenure faculty face, the stresses that they experience, and the satisfactions that sustain and motivate them, especially as they move toward tenure. Interest in acquiring a better understanding of the early career development of faculty has grown, however, with mounting evidence of a strong positive relationship between professional socialization and long-term job satisfaction, commitment, motivation, and productivity (Dean, 1983; Jones, 1983, 1986).

In 1986, a large public research university began a longitudinal study of one cohort of new faculty (Olsen, 1991; Sorcinelli, 1988). The goal of the study was to better understand the development of faculty careers in the period before tenure, as well as the ways in which faculty need change. Tasks that have become routine by year five of an appointment, for example, may consume substantial time and emotional energy in year one. Conversely, a vague concern about reappointment in year one may become an all-consuming pressure in year five.

This chapter first depicts the experience of those new faculty over a period of five years, investigating in some detail the exigencies of the fifth year—the period immediately preceding tenure—as well as changes experienced over the five years. The chapter then offers suggestions for the development of pretenure faculty.

A Longitudinal Study of New Faculty

The major premise of this study was that we need to know more about how new faculty begin and then establish their careers.

Methods. During the first year, all new faculty who had entered tenure-track positions at the assistant professor level in 1986 took part in interviews (between one and three hours) and were asked to complete a career development questionnaire. The interviews and questionnaires provided information on career choice, roles and responsibilities, opportunities and constraints, as well as work and life away from work satisfactions. Interview and questionnaire formats were similar to those used in prior research with faculty (Sorcinelli, 1985) and are available from the authors.

All members of the cohort volunteered to participate in the study the first year; those who did not participate in following years had either left campus or were inaccessible because they were engaged in commitments off campus. Of the fifty-four faculty who participated in the first year of the study, forty-seven were reinterviewed in 1988 and forty-five in 1990, the third and fifth years of appointment, respectively. The profile of the sample remained stable over time despite expected attrition.

In terms of career advancement, 96 percent of the forty-five faculty interviewed in year five had not yet received tenure. Eighteen percent of the sample had attained the rank of associate by 1990. An equal percentage were terminating their university appointments by the end of the 1991 academic year.

Findings. Interview and questionnaire formats produced both qualitative and quantitative results. Because of the length and breadth of responses over the five years, only a preliminary analysis of this rich data base can be presented here. We focus on the following themes: changes over time in teaching, changes over time in research, perspectives on review and tenure, and work satisfactions and stresses over time.

Changes over Time in Teaching

New faculty noted several striking changes in teaching over the course of the first five years of their academic appointments.

Time Spent on Teaching Preparation Declines. Over the five-year period, the trend of junior faculty was to spend greater amounts of time on research and service and somewhat less time on teaching as their careers progressed. The reduction in teaching time appeared to reflect greater efficiency in lecture preparation and grading with experience. Not only did faculty report more proficiency at these tasks generally, but the number of new courses declined so that by year five, only 40 percent of faculty reported new teaching preparations, as compared to nearly 100 percent in year one. In contrast to preparation time, contact hours with students remained fairly constant and, in the case of graduate students, increased. Typically, faculty devoted one to four hours a week outside of class to undergraduates and five or more hours to graduate students.

Teaching Is Satisfying and Less Stressful than Research. Data on teaching activities were encouraging. Faculty reported positive student evaluations, greater confidence in their own abilities to teach, and relatively high levels of satisfaction. With a greater sense of self-assurance, faculty became markedly more introspective about their teaching, that is, they worried more about what it was they should teach, how best to teach, where the students were in terms of skills and abilities, and how to get students to think critically and creatively; and they were less bound to notes and class schedules and more likely to pursue "tangents" and invite questions. One faculty member remarked, "I'm more confident now. There are more days when I feel like I have something more to offer than less. The question I keep coming back to is—I only have so much time to spend with students—am I teaching the right things? Am I covering things that are significant and useful? Why am I teaching what I am teaching? I've gotten to a level where I can worry about such things." And other faculty responded along the same lines: "I enjoy teaching more and I am better at it. I have a better focus on what I want to teach. With more maturity there is more interaction in class. . . . I'm at a new plateau. Initially it was a struggle to get everything organized. Now I want to teach people to think."

While teaching was seen as less stressful than research, it was not, however, without pressures and frustrations. Faculty felt that much of the teaching stress that they experienced stemmed from their own standards and expectations, but they also cited time for class preparation, poorly prepared or unmotivated students, and new course preparations as sources of difficulty. In particular, a number of faculty indicated that, over time, large lecture courses with limited opportunities for student feedback made it difficult to maintain energy and enthusiasm in the classroom.

Furthermore, a number of the faculty indicated that they wished for greater rewards from teaching: "You could drop dead trying to be a good teacher and not be recognized. I'm more committed to teaching now. I'm also realizing more and more how dangerous it is to feel that way." While almost 60 percent of the sample responded that their professional interests "lean to" or were "heavily oriented toward" research, they also clearly felt that teaching should be given more weight in review and tenure decisions.

Changes over Time in Research

Over the first five years of their appointments, new faculty noted changes in their levels of commitment to and stress about research.

Time Spent on Research Steadily Increases. One-third of the sample indicated that their commitment to research had grown over the course of their five-year appointment. Almost half reported spending more time in research as their career progressed. Worries over productivity were not reflected in publication records. In the last year of the study, 90 percent had submitted papers for presentation or publication, 52 percent had submitted three or more papers, and 17 percent had submitted a book or monograph. Almost 40 percent of faculty already had a nontextbook accepted or published and virtually all faculty had at least one refereed article. Another 40 percent had external grant funds to support their research in the prior academic year.

Stress About Research Productivity and Support Heightens. If discussions of research did not evidence less enthusiasm, the overall tenor of their responses was certainly more anxious. Faculty appeared to be at a watershed in their research, feeling "ready to burst on the scene" and "I have hit my stride," and, at the same time, concerned about research productivity and, in certain disciplines, grant support. While almost 75 percent of faculty rated themselves as "very satisfied" with the quality of their research, less than 60 percent gave themselves equally high marks for quantity (42 percent rated themselves as only somewhat or not at all satisfied).

It is noteworthy that much of what faculty found most satisfying about research, for example, posing new questions, looking at problems in alternative ways, finding coherent patterns in disparate data, is very similar to the skills and abilities that they sought to inculcate in students through their teaching. While the relationship between research and teaching and their reciprocal benefits is often construed in terms of enrichment of content knowledge, it may be that the cognitive underpinnings of the research process shape instruction and pedagogical goals in even more telling ways.

In asking faculty about the nature of their research and their needs, it became clear that the greater demands for productivity had in turn made a variety of resources essential to the task of conducting research. Faculty regularly reported the need for additional research assistants or technicians, collaborators with specific equipment or expertise, and computer equipment—lap-top computers for work in distant archives, mainframe computers adequate to deal with massive data sets or complex statistical models, or simply personal computers for word processing. Several faculty noted that their failure to secure these resources early in their appointments had severely undermined their research and chances for tenure. In some cases, faculty felt that they were naive about how to obtain needed funds and equipment, whereas a few others felt that the department or institution was an obstacle. As sources of external support grow fewer and more selective and research needs accelerate, institutional and individual ability to provide necessary research support will depend on more timely, more explicit, and more collaborative strategies.

Perspectives on Review and Tenure

At the end of year one, most new faculty were hard-pressed to provide concrete information on tenure requirements, their ability to meet these requirements, and feedback on their performance. By year five, approximately 58 percent of the faculty anticipating tenure review indicated that they were "quite" or "totally" confident of their ability to meet the requirements for tenure. About one-half of the faculty felt that tenure standards were clear. However, many felt that tenure review had become more stringent in the past several years and that its criteria and procedures required better definition and clearer communication. In general, faculty felt more assured of a thorough and fair assessment at the departmental level than at higher administrative levels.

More Explicit, Regular, and Positive Feedback Requested. When asked, 40 percent of the sample indicated that their most recent review had been "not at all" or only "somewhat" fair. In particular, one-half of the faculty respondents felt that departmental colleagues' evaluations of their work could be communicated more effectively and that more specific suggestions for improvement were needed. The written evaluations provided each year by many departments were a particular source of irritation. A number of faculty felt that the neutrality of the language and the routine qualification of positive statements in the evaluations were designed to serve more as an insurance policy for the university than as feedback for the faculty member. One faculty member described the situation this way: "It's like trying to make a commitment to a potential spouse who does not want to make a commitment. It's hard to make a commitment when it is a one-way street."

When asked to characterize how departmental colleagues evaluated their work, the concern over quantity of research and, for certain faculty, external funding was again apparent. The faculty estimated that the number of refereed journal articles necessary for tenure was, on average, 7, a figure slightly lower than the average level of actual productivity reported by the fifth year, 10.5 articles. About 33 percent of faculty also indicated that a book or monograph was needed, although 39 percent actually had produced books that were either already published or accepted for publication.

If the faculty are correct about the research requirements and their own productivity, it would appear that the relative confidence of the more than one-half of respondents anticipating tenure review was well founded. This is not to say, of course, that more explicit, regular, and positive feedback is not needed for the almost equal percentage of faculty who expressed concerns about the quality of feedback, particularly in the case of those who may be less clear about professional priorities at the outset of their careers or whose prior training and background is less traditional for the academy.

More Emphasis on Teaching in Review and Tenure Desired. Perhaps one of the most striking findings of the present study and other recent investigations is the greater weight that faculty wish to see ascribed to teaching in tenure and review decisions. Faculty were asked to rate the importance of eleven different criteria in "actual" tenure decisions and the "ideal" importance that should be attached to these criteria. A comparison of real and ideal ratings showed that faculty concurred with the emphasis placed on publications ("actual" mean rating of 3.66 and "ideal" mean rating of 3.75 on a 5-point scale). However, it was clear that faculty felt that current assessments severely undervalued teaching ("actual" mean rating of 2.23 and "ideal" mean rating of 3.52). Data suggest that faculty wish to weight instruction more heavily because of their personal investment of time and energy, because they feel that their teaching is generally well received by students and colleagues, and because many have a firm commitment to the teaching mission of the university.

Work Satisfactions and Stresses over Time

Faculty in their first, third, and fifth years of appointment were asked a series of general and then more specific questions about the satisfactions and stresses of their academic positions. We were not surprised to find that work stress increased with the greater immediacy of tenure. However, it was less clear a priori that work satisfaction would show a corresponding decline over the same time period. Levels of work satisfaction and work stress have shown a moderate negative correlation in general samples of workers. However, faculty differ from other workers and even other professional groups in the extent to which their job satisfaction derives from the intrinsic aspects of the work (Austin and Gamson, 1983). Because intrinsic rewards are determined by the individual in relation to the nature of the work, it would be reasonable to expect faculty satisfaction to be more stable and less subject to the vagaries of external factors and stresses. Earlier studies have indicated that faculty tend to exhibit both high levels of stress and satisfaction (Sorcinelli, 1988). The literature on stress suggests that this covariation is in part attributable to high levels of support and autonomy that help individuals "buffer" or "cope with" the negative effects of fairly heavy work stress and promote job satisfaction (La Rocco and Jones, 1978; Lefcourt, Martin, and Salek, 1984; Thoits, 1986).

Intrinsic Rewards Remain Strong but Work Satisfaction Declines. Our data indicated that faculty satisfaction with the intrinsic rewards of an academic career remained strong and consistent. Thus, for example, faculty evidenced consistently high levels of satisfaction with the autonomy that their career provided, the opportunities for intellectual discovery and growth, and the sense of accomplishment. At the same time, the data showed a significant decrease in overall job satisfaction over the five-year period.

A Downward Turn in Collegiality and Social Support. The greatest declines in satisfaction were with support and recognition for both teaching and scholarship and by both colleagues and administrators. The faculty felt more satisfied with the recognition that they received from their discipline than from their campus.

It seems reasonable to assume that the faculty grew more dissatisfied with the support and recognition received from departmental colleagues and university administrators as they anticipated a lengthy and arduous review of their work carried out by these same individuals. But, at the same time, few areas of academic life are more central than collegiality and working in a community of scholars. In earlier research on this data set, "support of faculty colleagues" was found to be closely associated with many of the intrinsic rewards that are the mainstay of the academic career (Olsen, 1991). Thus, the question of whether a declining sense of collegial support simply represents growing anxiety over upcoming evaluation and review, whether it signals a more general deterioration of faculty relations, or both, is worth careful consideration. In addition, the issue of collegial support is particularly germane at tenure, a time of acutely high stress in a faculty career. Research on work stress has shown that social support, particularly from colleagues within the workplace, can help mitigate a number of the negative consequences of stress and improve work performance (Billings and Moos, 1982; Ganster, Fusilier, and Mayes, 1986).

Collegiality Sought Outside of Department and Off Campus. When asked whether their respective departments are good places to work, 66 percent of faculty responded that their departments were better than average, and 56 percent that their departments were good to excellent. However, faculty, on average, rated colleagues outside their departments as most helpful or supportive of their careers, with untenured faculty and chairpersons as next most supportive, respectively. Tenured faculty and deans were seen as least helpful and supportive.

Consistent with data suggesting greater recognition and collegial support from outside the university, about one-third of faculty reported contact with outside colleagues at least once a week, and almost one-half indicated such communications at least one a month. In contrast to the close, frequent contacts that many faculty had established outside the university, over one-third indicated that none of the senior faculty in their departments had ever been particularly interested in or helpful to them in their careers, and almost one-half indicated that they had expected more support and guidance from senior faculty than were received. One participant remarked, "Basically the senior faculty told me to go into my office, close the door, and pound on the computer until tenure." And another explained, "A lot of the stress is because you don't have any sense of what is enough. You need some sense of where you stand from a senior person, a mentor. . . . You always tend to go into the most challenging area and it would be helpful to have someone to speak to about the trade-offs, et cetera. Not so much a formal meeting but a social context and the rest would come out of it."

More Guidance from Senior Colleagues Desired. One of the potential implications of a lack of senior faculty support is that junior faculty fail to receive very specific and vital forms of help and guidance. Faculty were asked about the types of support—resources, advice, opportunities, and so on—provided by chairs, deans, junior and senior colleagues, and colleagues outside the university. Data suggest that the support provided by different groups of individuals varies markedly. Junior colleagues are an important source of emotional support, but senior faculty are looked to for advice, answers to professional questions, and critical review of grant proposals and papers. Pretenure faculty who reported that they could not rely on senior colleagues for this kind of help felt disadvantaged and often turned to colleagues elsewhere and even students to fill the void. "I've trained my own research colleagues," said one faculty member. It is questionable, however, whether students or distant collaborators can socialize junior faculty or promote their career development as effectively as can senior colleagues in the same department and institution.

Increased Incidence of Work Stress Reported. The proportion of faculty who characterized their work lives as "very stressful" rose dramatically: from 33 percent in 1986, to 49 percent in 1988, and to 71 percent in 1990. These figures are in contrast to the 15 percent of faculty who assigned a rating of "very stressful" to their nonwork lives all three years. Moreover, the impact of work life on nonwork life was perceived as extremely negative. As noted earlier, the greatest stress appeared to stem from pressure for research productivity, time constraints, and the balancing of teaching, research, and service commitments.

It was expected that faculty would experience greater work stress with the approach of tenure. The question of what specific effects the heightened level of stress would have on faculty was less clear. Work stress has been shown to be associated with poor health, negative affect, a loss of motivation, and, in more severe cases, depression (Ganster, Fusilier, and Mayes, 1986; La Rocco, House, and French, 1980). Obviously, any of these outcomes would be highly undesirable at a time when faculty need to be highly effective and productive professionally.

In fact, 41 percent of faculty indicated that their health had deteriorated over the prior five years. About 50 percent felt that their health had remained stable, and less than 10 percent indicated that it had improved. The kinds of health-related problems that faculty were most likely to report were weight gain, loss of stamina, and low-grade chronic illnesses.

When asked specifically about pretenure anxieties, one-third of faculty reported that they were "often" or "very often" worried about being evaluated on the bases of irrelevant criteria, annoying or offending a tenured colleague, being unclear about what colleagues thought of them, and the possibility of losing their jobs. Although the faculty were worried and over-burdened by the demands of their careers and the impending tenure reviews, however, they did not appear to be dispirited or to lack enthusiasm for their work. Faculty reported that they often felt overwhelmed and were sometimes exhausted and anxious. It was more rare that they were uninterested in their work, indecisive, bitter, or depressed. On the contrary, they indicated that they often felt excited by their work, friendly toward their colleagues, and even at times highly energetic.

Thus, the picture of this group is perhaps as positive as one can expect given the rigors of the tenure process and the magnitude of its implications. Faculty health does suffer somewhat from the long hours of work and unending demands for productivity. At the same time, faculty energy and morale are sustained by interest in and commitment to their research and teaching and the intrinsic rewards that they reap from fulfillment of these tasks.

Suggestions for the Development of Pretenure Faculty

Several overriding and interrelated themes emerged from these longitudinal data. First, while pretenure faculty consistently placed a high value on the autonomous and growth-enhancing aspects of their careers, we also found a downward turn in faculty work satisfaction and an increased incidence of work stress over time. Results suggest that the support and recognition for both teaching and scholarship given to pretenure faculty by both colleagues and administrators may be crucial to their professional development.

Second, pretenure faculty reported a diminished sense of collegiality over time and expressed a critical need for more extensive, open collegial relations among faculty, especially between junior and senior faculty. While the fostering of collegiality is not a simple task, there does not appear to be a better way to socialize pretenure faculty than through the advice and guidance of more experienced colleagues. More fluid relations between junior and senior colleagues could provide more and better information about the culture of the institution, teaching and research opportunities, the tenure process, and feedback about performance and means of improvement.

Third, and related to issues of satisfaction and collegial support, is the issue of rewards for teaching. Pretenure faculty felt that teaching should constitute a key criterion for tenure. Faculty commitment to teaching, as demonstrated by the time spent on their courses and on meetings with students, belies the notion that many pretenure faculty sacrifice their teaching to gain time for research. The data also suggest that pretenure faculty would benefit from working with senior faculty or teaching consultants, particularly in large lecture classes.

What is remarkable about the present set of findings is the level of commitment that the faculty demonstrated to the personal and intellectual rewards of their profession—even in the face of tenure anxiety, rigorous review, and little guidance from senior colleagues. Still, present forums do not appear to provide the kind of collegial, intellectual, and supportive environments that best encourage professional socialization.

Subsequent chapters in this volume suggest an array of responses—orientations, mentoring, and research and teaching resources—that can help senior colleagues, departments, and institutions better socialize pretenure faculty. Yet, our findings reveal that the key to support of pretenure faculty lies not only in institutional programs but also in what one junior faculty referred to as "social context." Put simply, we need to cultivate the kind of milieu in which an understanding of expectations and professional values can grow.

The approach to socialization advocated here turns the pretenure process away from the concerns of correctly deciphering a preordained set of criteria, casting about for professional contacts, or hiding teaching or research problems from senior colleagues for fear that these troubles will be viewed as inadequacies at review time. Instead, the process is recast in terms of establishing oneself as an accomplished scholar and teacher based on achievements mutually valued by the individual and the university community. This approach has the added benefit of providing the kind of social support, sense of autonomy, and control that help minimize the inevitable stress of the pretenure years and promote productivity and loyalty to the institution.

References

Austin, A. E., and Gamson, Z. F. *Academic Workplace: New Demands, Heightened Tensions.* ASHE-ERIC Higher Education Research Reports, no. 10. Washington, D.C.: Association for the Study of Higher Education, 1983.

Billings, A. G., and Moos, R. H. "Work Stress and Stress-Buffering Roles of Work and Family Resources." *Journal of Occupational Behavior,* 1982, *3,* 215–232.

Boice, R. "New Faculty as Teachers." *Journal of Higher Education,* 1991, *62* (2), 150–173.

Dean, R. "Reality Shock: The Link Between Socialization and Organizational Commitment." *Journal of Management Development,* 1983, *2,* 55–65.

Fink, L. D. (ed.). *The First Year of College Teaching.* New Directions for Teaching and Learning, no. 17. San Francisco: Jossey-Bass, 1984.

Ganster, D. C., Fusilier, M. R., and Mayes, B. T. "Role of Social Support in the Experience of Stress at Work." *Journal of Applied Psychology,* 1986, *71,* 102–110.

Jones, G. R. "Psychological Orientation and the Process of Organizational Socialization: An Interactionist Perspective." *Academy of Management Review,* 1983, *8,* 464–474.

Jones, G. R. "Socialization Tactics, Self-Efficacy, and Newcomers' Adjustments to Organizations." *Academy of Management Journal,* 1986, *29,* 262–279.

La Rocco, J. M., House, S., and French, J. R. "Social Support, Occupational Stress, and Health." *Journal of Health and Social Behavior,* 1980, *21,* 202–218.

La Rocco, J. M., and Jones, A. P. "Co-Worker and Leader Support as Moderators of Stress-Strain Relationships in Work Situations." *Journal of Applied Psychology,* 1978, *63,* 629–634.

Lefcourt, H. M., Martin, R. A., and Salek, W. E. "Locus of Control and Social Support: Interactive Moderators of Stress." *Journal of Personality and Social Psychology,* 1984, *47,* 378–389.

Olsen, D. "Work Satisfaction and Stress in the First and Third Years of Academic Appointment." Unpublished manuscript, Indiana University, 1991.

Sorcinelli, M. D. "Faculty Careers: Personal, Institutional, and Societal Dimensions." Paper presented at the 69th annual meeting of the American Educational Research Association, Chicago, March 1985.

Sorcinelli, M. D. "Satisfactions and Concerns of New University Teachers." *To Improve the Academy,* 1988, *7,* 121–131.

Thoits, P. A. "Social Support as Coping Assistance." *Journal of Consulting and Clinical Psychology,* 1986, *54,* 416–423.

Turner, J. L., and Boice, R. "Starting at the Beginning: Concerns and Needs of New Faculty." *To Improve the Academy,* 1987, *6,* 41–55.

Whitt, E. J. " 'Hit the Ground Running': Experiences of New Faculty in a School of Education." *Review of Higher Education,* 1991, *14* (2), 177–197.

DEBORAH OLSEN is director of faculty development in the Office for Academic Affairs, Indiana University, Bloomington.

MARY DEANE SORCINELLI is director of the Center for Teaching and associate adjunct professor in the Division of Educational Policy and Administration, University of Massachusetts, Amherst.

*Studies of stress among new and junior faculty identify sources of
tension and strategies for controlling careers in the early years.*

New and Junior Faculty Stress:
Research and Responses

Mary Deane Sorcinelli

An interesting paradox can be found in the literature on new and junior
faculty. Nearly all newcomers report high levels of satisfaction with their
careers. When asked to identify aspects of academic life that consistently
afford satisfaction, most new faculty describe their work as providing personal autonomy, a sense of accomplishment, the capacity to have an impact
on others, and the opportunity for personal and intellectual growth (Turner
and Boice, 1989; Sorcinelli, 1988). At the same time, however, virtually all
of the same faculty rate their work as stressful. Words such as *tension,
pressure, anxiety,* and *worry* stand out in an even cursory reading of the
literature (Fink, 1984; Turner and Boice, 1989; Sorcinelli, 1988; Whitt, 1991).

Unfortunately, the tensions of the first year do not appear to be offset
by experience. As reported in detail in Olsen and Sorcinelli (this volume),
a colleague and I have followed the career development of one cohort of
new faculty over a five-year period via interviews and questionnaires (Sorcinelli, 1988; Olsen, 1990). Our longitudinal study found that the proportion of newcomers reporting their work life as *very* stressful rose
dramatically, and even among highly satisfied individuals, work stress
steadily eroded satisfaction.

While life can be stressful for all academics, researchers also have
noted that untenured faculty report higher levels of stress than do their
tenured colleagues. In a national study of 1,920 faculty members at 80
doctoral-granting institutions, Gmelch, Wilke, and Lovrich (1986) found
that five distinct dimensions of stress appeared throughout the academic
career. It is particularly noteworthy that there were statistically significant
differences between tenured and untenured faculty in each of the five

dimensions investigated. A subsequent national survey of 3,928 faculty at 392 two- and four-year colleges and universities also found that untenured faculty membrs as a whole reported more stress than did tenured faculty on all investigated factors (Dey, 1990). Taken together, single-year, longitudinal, qualitative, and survey research all concur that academic stress impinges heavily on untenured faculty.

What aspects of academic life trigger the levels of tension that newcomers feel and experience? In this chapter, we identify some of the major stresses reported by untenured faculty. We draw from the literature both on new and junior faculty and on academic stress. Although factors of stress are clustered somewhat differently across the studies, several dimensions appear consistently in both literatures. We also track changes in stresses over several years by drawing on our five-year study of a single cohort of new faculty as well as on a four-year study of several successively hired cohorts of new faculty (Boice, 1991a, 1991b). The chapter concludes with suggestions for providing more support and direction for new faculty.

Stress Point One: Not Enough Time

The predominant source of stress reported in nearly all studies of new faculty stems primarily from the press of finding enough time to get everything done (Turner and Boice, 1989; Fink, 1984; Sorcinelli, 1988; Whitt, 1991). "Not enough time to do my work" ranks as one of the major contributors to stress among new faculty who describe their semesters as fragmented by too many tasks and too little time to complete them.

Demanding workloads and difficulties in balancing new teaching and research responsibilities nearly always head the list of complaints. Fink (1984) interviewed new faculty and reported that they had difficulty juggling pressures for publication with heavy teaching loads. Similarly, Sorcinelli (1988) and Turner and Boice (19890 described stresses related to the demand to meet long-term goals for research (writing several articles, finishing a book, getting a laboratory up and running) versus the immediate and unpostponable demands of preparing for classes.

For some new faculty, the effects of such daily tension are debilitating. In interviews with new faculty, Reynolds (1988) found ill health a problem for over one-half of her respondents. Sorcinelli (1988) found that despite their remarkable capacity for sustaining grueling schedules, new faculty described bouts of fatigue, feelings of failure, marital tensions, and frequent illnesses. Turner and Boice (1989) documented similar effects. A majority (83 percent) of their sample of new faculty described a level of "busyness" during the first year that resulted in physical and emotional symptoms (for example, fatigue, insomnia, and anxiety attacks).

In addition, the concern of new faculty about lack of time and balance is the most consistent source of stress over time. Our study found that by the fifth year junior faculty members described an increased personal comfort with teaching as well as greater clarity and direction in their research agendas. At the same time, however, satisfaction with the ability to find enough time to do work and to balance the conflicting demands of research, teaching, and service continued to decline. Nearly one-half of our respondents also reported a concomitant deterioration of their health.

Stress Point Two: Inadequate Feedback and Recognition

Another factor that produces considerable stress among new and junior faculty is inadequate feedback, recognition, and reward. Several studies on academic stress have found that faculty members across career stages express tension about such issues as unclear criteria for evaluating research, teaching, and service; inadequate university recognition for their contributions; and insufficient financial rewards (Gmelch, 1987; Gmelch, Wilke, and Lovrich, 1986; Melendez and de Guzman, 1983; Seldin, 1987).

There is some evidence that stresses related to the dimension of feedback and recognition are felt most keenly by new and junior faculty members. For example, several studies of first-year faculty conclude that early formal evaluations are significant contributors to faculty stress. In our study, first-year faculty members described the reappointment process as daunting. They reported both exhaustion and stress as they cast about collecting evaluations (for example, on grant efforts, manuscripts, teaching) and contemplated facing year after year of rigorous review. One new faculty member explained, "In this blur, one is arrested twice each year by the need to document and defend one's performance. One cycle, set of forms, and instructions for the purposes of conferring merit salary and another for reappointment." New faculty recommended that departments consider more supportive, informal reviews for the first year (Sorcinelli, 1988).

The particular stress of teaching evaluations is worth special mention. In a two-year study of new faculty as teachers, Boice (1991b) found that they taught cautiously and defensively so as to avoid public failures at teaching. He reported that new faculty "routinely worried aloud about criticisms of their teaching, especially the sort that would earn repeated listings in reports of tenure committees" (1991b, p. 171). Boice recommended that departments safeguard new faculty from all formal evaluations of classroom performance for a year or two.

Over the five years of our study, we were able to take a careful look at faculty concerns about evaluation as well as broader issues related to recognition and reward. Often by the third year, and certainly by the fifth year, junior faculty had undergone several departmental reviews, and the department and university had taken on a more complex role in combining support and evaluation (Olsen, 1990). It was disheartening but not entirely surprising to find that from year one to year five our cohort reported a steadily eroding level of satisfaction with feedback on how they were doing, support received from the administration, recognition of their work by the university, participation in decision making, and salary.

Stress Point Three: Unrealistic Expectations

Faculty members have been well schooled in the ethos of academic success. Many view research, publications, grants, and presentations of papers as highly important and even essential to advancement, rewards, and recognition. A sense of failure in the academic arena, then, can set a foundation for faculty stress.

Gmelch, Wilke, and Lovrich (1986) found that worries about "professional identity" were a dominant factor of stress. Faculty also acknowledged that they had a tendency to set excessively high self-expectations, thus heightening anxiety about achieving desired levels of accomplishment. Gmelch and his colleagues discovered, in fact, that it was not so much the absolute amount of success achieved by faculty members but rather the relationship between level of achievement and personal aspirations that caused their stress.

Studies of first-year faculty conclude that newcomers feel a great deal of self-imposed pressure to perform well on every front. In our study, virtually all new faculty had set extremely high goals for their first year—in both teaching and research—and then felt doubt when they did not measure up: "It's been very stressful to try to do everything and do it well. I'm not coping very well and I work every living, breathing moment I'm awake. . . . The problem is that I could live with less than a perfect job as a student but not as a professor."

Whitt (1991) found not only that new faculty set excessively high self-expectations but also that deans and chairs shared and reinforced those goals. Both department chairs and deans expected new faculty to settle in, learn their way around, focus on their goals, and manage a multiplicity of tasks in a short amount of time. In her interviews, Whitt heard one phrase so often from both new faculty and administrators that it became tantamount to a slogan: "Hit the ground running."

Even over time, new faculty are not immune to their own and others' expectations; they not only hit the ground running but also keep on running. In our longitudinal study, we noted that after five years in their positions, junior faculty still worried about the quantity and quality of their research, even though many had met or exceeded departmental and institutional demands for productivity. They also expressed continuing concern about their departmental colleagues' evaluations of their work, and about keeping up with standards set by colleagues both in and outside of the university.

Stress Point Four: Lack of Collegiality

A number of research studies on the sources of stress among professors cite unsatisfactory relations with faculty colleagues. Melendez and de Guzman (1983) and Seldin (1987) found that a predominant aspect of stress from interactions with colleagues was the lack of respect and rapport among faculty due, in part, to political divisions and professional jealousies. Gmelch (1987) suggested that faculty face additional stress in their relations with department chairs.

Investigators of new faculty have noted that collegiality is a high priority but is less than satisfactorily achieved. Fink (1984) first documented the need for more support by peers of new college teachers. When first-year faculty were asked for recommendations for their own institutions, two-thirds said that they would have appreciated more assistance from fellow faculty members. Types of assistance most desired included support for teaching (for example, resources and peer visits to class) and more discussion of criteria used in salary and personnel decisions.

Sorcinelli (1988), Turner and Boice (1989), and Whitt (1991) found similar concerns. New faculty reported the lack of collegial relations as the most surprising and disappointing aspect of their first year. Few faculty engaged in the kind of conversations with colleagues about scholarship, teaching, and other work-related activities that they had hoped for. Collaboration in research (for example, reading a manuscript or grant proposal) or in teaching (for example, visiting a classroom) also were infrequent.

New faculty do report one element of satisfaction among the stresses of collegiality: the supportive role often played by department chairs. Sorcinelli (1988) and Turner and Boice (1989) found that new faculty identified their chairpersons as advocates and, in some cases, the most important individuals during their first year. Chairs cited as particularly helpful took time to assign courses that fit faculty interests, negotiated minimal new course preparations or reduced loads, secured internal funds for travel or resources, and provided guidance for annual reviews. In contrast, chairs who assigned excessive workloads and provided little mentoring to new faculty were a dominant source of stress.

Investigators have posited several explanations for new faculty members' dissatisfaction with collegiality. Over the last decade, departments have become more diverse—in gender, race, life-style, age, training, sense of mission, priorities, and salaries. Such diversity may exacerbate the sense of separateness that new faculty feel from senior colleagues (Reynolds, 1988; Sorcinelli, 1989; Whitt, 1991). In addition, Turner and Boie (1989) and Whitt (1991) found that new faculty were surprisingly passive about taking the initiative in interacting with colleagues. They rarely sought help, advice, or mentoring. Finally, new faculty may have unrealistic expectations of their chairs and colleagues. Whitt (1991) separately interviewed six new faculty and their respective chairs. She found that department chairs saw themselves as more helpful (for example, answering questions and anticipating concerns) than did the new faculty.

What kinds of changes occur in sense of collegiality over time? Two longitudinal studies provide different takes on the problem yet draw similar conclusions. In his study of collegiality in four successive cohorts of new faculty, Boice (1991a) reported that by their fourth year on campus new faculty found improvements in collegial support and intellectual stimulation. Also, in comparing the four cohorts, Boice found that collegial climate seemed to have improved for the last two groups of new hires. He concluded that the socialization process of new faculty was longer and more complex than previously suggested. Over time, junior faculty seemed to have adjusted their expectations for collegial support and taken some initiative in seeking out senior faculty who could be helpful. In addition, the campus, which had not hired many new faculty in over a decade, may have slowly become more cognizant of the needs of new faculty.

Our longitudinal study also paid special attention to changes in perceptions of collegiality. The findings are equally intriguing. First, we were encouraged to find that lack of collegial support declined as a stress point after the first year. But we were perplexed to find that faculty actually felt less satisfied over time with the support received from their colleagues (Olsen, 1990). The importance of this finding was underscored by the fact that collegial support was of increasing significance to the respondents' work satisfaction over time.

Clearly, the need for the support of colleagues had not declined in importance over the five years. In fact, Olsen (1990) suggests that collegial relations were of at least equal importance but seemingly of a different nature. In the first year, for example, new faculty experienced greater stress when they felt less support from their colleagues. Olsen speculates that by years three and five, however, new faculty had either developed networks beyond campus to offset isolation or simply let go of the ideal of a work environment characterized by collaboration. Over the same semesters, however, they became less fulfilled as they sought, but did not find, the enrichment of a community of scholars in their home departments or institution. Certainly, both our findings and those of Boice suggest that, over time, new faculty would benefit significantly from more collegial, intellectually supportive environments.

Stress Point Five: Balancing Work and Life Outside of Work

As noted earlier, numerous researchers have indicated that the tensions produced by the conflicting demands of professional tasks—teaching, writing, staying current in one's field, advising, securing grants, and serving the university and profession—are a principal source of stress for new faculty. Research also suggests that efforts to balance the demands of professional work and personal life—being a spouse, a parent, a child of aging parents, an involved citizen—may compound new faculty stress.

In studies of faculty development across career stages (Peters and Mayfield, 1982; Sorcinelli, 1985; Sorcinelli and Near, 1989), researchers found that approximately one-half of the faculty members interviewed or surveyed reported considerable stress in trying to balance the needs and duties of personal and family life and the requirements of professional success. Research by the Carnegie Foundation for the Advancement of Teaching (1986) also indicated that the extent to which work intruded into personal life was a primary factor in influcing overall dissatisfaction among faculty members.

But what about new and junior faculty? If demography is destiny, new faculty are already facing and will continue to face pressures in juggling career and family life. Finkelstein and LaCelle-Peterson (this volume) review evidence of a rise in both dual-career couples and commuter marriages among junior faculty. There is also evidence of a rise in female junior faculty who have chosen *not* to forgo or defer having children, unlike the stereotypically unmarried and childless academic woman (Levinson, Tolle, and Lewis, 1989; Sorcinelli and Gregory, 1987).

In previous work with a sample of untenured and tenured faculty, we found that junior faculty reported significantly more "negative spillover" (their work lives negatively "spilled over" into their personal lives) than did associate or full professors (Sorcinelli and Near, 1989). In our longitudinal study, we decided to look at the occurrence of spillover over time. During the first year, new faculty decribed negative spillover between time and energy for work and for spouses, children, dual careers, and commuter relationships. They also cited conflicts between work and leisure activities. Lack of time and energy for exercise, reading, hobbies, and social and civic activities were common concerns (Sorcinelli, 1988).

Presumably, new faculty find ways to resolve tensions and to better balance work and life away from work over time. Our longitudinal data, however, provide mixed findings on rate of success here. We were encouraged to find that, by year three, new faculty were actively negotiating conflicts between work and life outside of work (Olsen and Stage, 1990). This finding is reinforced by Boice's (1991a) study of four successive cohorts of new faculty. By year four, he found that new faculty had taken concrete steps to reduce negative spillover and had detailed specific plans for community- or family-based activities.

At the same time, our data also indicated that over time faculty became less satisfied with the balance achieved between their work and nonwork lives. In particular, there was an increase in the percentage of junior faculty indicating that their work lives had a substantial negative impact on their nonwork lives. The conflict stemmed largely from "an erosion of leisure time and social relations under the press of institutional and self-imposed work commitments" (Olsen, 1990, p. 8).

In sum, findings suggest that new faculty continue to experience stresses and strains due to the demands of work and nonwork roles throughout the years before tenure. For many newcomers, the goal of striking an acceptable long-term balance between these two significant domains of their lives may take considerable time to achieve.

Personal Coping Strategies

What strategies can new faculty members employ to deal with academic stress? The question is especially important for the junior members of the academic community since, for them, success or failure at developing adequate coping strategies will determine the quality of their lives for the next twenty-five to thirty-five years. A place to start is at the individual level. Research on stress teaches that if individuals can identify their stressors and learn strategies to respond positively, they can begin to manage their own stress effectively (Gmelch, 1987).

We have consulted with hundreds of new and junior faculty and they have offered many useful suggestions for personal stress management. Also, there are several helpful articles, books, and videotapes on managing time and academic stress (Seldin, 1987; *Coping with Academic Stress,* 1989; Zanna and Darley, 1987). The following are ten guidelines for managing time, setting realistic goals, getting rewards, finding support, and balancing work and life away from work.

Prioritize to Identify the Value of Projects. As individuals, what are the most important things that we should be doing? What can each of us let drop (our personal safety valves)? We must carefully consider the value of each project and task to determine "crucial" versus "backburner" demands. If need be, actually rank tasks in numerical order of priority. Find ways to keep priorities in mind—a manilla file of goals organized from high to low priority, index cards of projects, courses, and students, and so on.

Set Realistic Goals as a First Step Toward Reaching the Ideal. New faculty often entertain excessively high self-expectations. Do not say yes or no when asked to take on another responsibility. Instead, take a day to ponder the matter. Consider what needs to happen to complete the obligation (for example, timing, staffing, deadlines, costs, shifting other work and family commitments). Decide how many articles, projects, students, committees can be juggled simultaneously and say NO when the limits are exceeded.

Use Organizing Techniques to Get Control of Work Time. The structure that one creates for oneself must be made concrete. Draw up a daily "to do" list to help prioritize important tasks. Use an appointment book that demarcates large time frames (for example, week, month, year) as well as each day. Never schedule more than a half-day of activities so that the urgent conversation or last-minute crisis can be accommodated.

Know and Capitalize on One's Own Prime Time. Each of us have hours when we are at our best. We need to save our best hours for high-priority tasks such as reading, writing, and preparing classes. The office can be made off-limits for those periods of time by closing the door, putting up a "Please Don't Disturb" sign, and turning on the telephone answering machine to deflect interruptions.

Find Alternative Work Space to Avoid Interruptions. What may take several hours to accomplish at the office can often be done in a minimal amount of time in a quieter environment. If the library or home is a more ideal setting for a complicated project, consider working there for a half- or whole day each week.

Initiate Relaxation Exercises to Restore Energy. When tension builds, take a few minutes to relax body and mind. For example, close the eyes, take three deep breaths, and then imagine being in a place that represents calm. Try to experience this place with all of the senses. Once relaxed, return to work with renewed energy and focus.

Change Work Style to Enhance a Sense of Well-Being. When confronted with a full schedule of appointments, the temptation is to skip lunch. Rethink that strategy. Skipped meals, especially lunch, lead to mid-afternoon fatigue. Make time for a sandwich, a ten-minute walk across campus. On a larger scale, make time to exercise, stop smoking, and reduce fat, caffeine, salt, and sugar intake.

Cultivate a Coping Philosophy to Overcome Pressures. To deal with tension and time pressures, cultivate not only coping strategies but also a relaxed state of mind. New faculty describe internal conversations in which they tell themselves that it will not be disastrous if the journal article goes out in January rather than December, if memos needing responses pile up during a busy week, if the house is not immaculate, if their children do not receive quality time at all times.

Seek Social Support on and off the Campus. Research shows that stress levels are lower for professionals who share their problems with others (for example, spouse or colleagues). Take time to learn from colleagues—stop at a colleague's office for a chat and attend informal departmental gatherings. Set aside time for leisure and family. Schedule one weekend away, or at least one cultural or social activity each semester. For example, some junior faculty find it helpful to buy tickets to concerts or basketball games ahead of time so that they are compelled to go. Some dual-career couples with children schedule monthly lunches or daily telephone calls—just to talk.

Reward Oneself for Working Hard at a Demanding Career. What are an academic's billable hours? Pay attention to "in-come" as well as "out-go." The activities of commuting, advising students, lunching with a colleague, reading, attending faculty meetings, and preparing classes are work. Often, our real work is invisible and feedback is delayed. We need to give generous estimates of time spent on our careers and reward ourselves with time off—cook a meal, read a huge novel, go shopping.

Institutional Actions

While some of the responsibility for stress management belongs to the individual, it is also clear that no personal coping strategy is adequate to solve the problems of new and junior faculty stress as they now exist. Personal strategies can make a difference but certainly not all of the difference. Solutions also require changes among the demands, structures, policies, and values of disciplines and institutions.

Institutions can do much to create environments that encourage and model balance for new faculty. The programs and strategies outlined in this volume provide a good beginning. New faculty orientations and programs to support mentoring, research and teaching, and training for department chairs are important places to start. Solutions to the deeper tensions among the issues of roles and responsibilities, rewards and recognition, collegiality, and career and personal life are more difficult to achieve. But these are the issues that colleges and universities will need to address if they hope to attract and keep bright young people in the academic profession.

References

Boice, R. "New Faculty as Colleagues." *International Journal of Qualitative Studies in Education,* 1991a, 4 (1), 29–44.

Boice, R. "New Faculty as Teachers." *Journal of Higher Education,* 1991b, 62 (2), 150–173.

Carnegie Foundation for the Advancement of Teaching. "The Satisfied Faculty." *Change Magazine,* Mar.-Apr. 1986, pp. 31–34.

Coping with Academic Stress. Videotape series. Madison: College of Agricultural and Life Sciences, University of Wisconsin, 1989.

Dey, E. L. "Dimensions of Faculty Stress: Evidence from a Recent National Survey." Paper presented at the annual meeting of the Association for the Study of Higher Education, Portland, Oregon, November 1990.

Fink, L. D. (ed.). *The First Year of College Teaching.* New Directions for Teaching and Learning, no. 17. San Francisco: Jossey-Bass, 1984.

Gmelch, W. H. "What Colleges and Universities Can Do About Faculty Stressors." In P. Seldin (ed.), *Coping with Faculty Stress.* New Directions for Teaching and Learning, no. 29. San Francisco: Jossey-Bass, 1987.

Gmelch, W. H., Wilke, P. K., and Lovrich, N. P. "Dimensions of Stress Among University Faculty." *Research in Higher Education,* 1986, 24 (3), 266–286.

Levinson, W., Tolle, S. W., and Lewis, C. "Women in Academic Medicine: Combining Career and Family." *New England Journal of Medicine,* 1989, 321, 1511–1517.

Melendez, W. A., and de Guzman, R. M. *Burnout: The New Academic Disease.* ASHE-ERIC Higher Education Research Reports, no. 9. Washington, D.C.: Association for the Study of Higher Education, 1983.

Olsen, D. "Work Satisfaction and Stress in the First and Third Years of Academic Appoint-ment." Paper presented at the annual meeting of the Association for the Study of Higher Education, Portland, Oregon, November 1990.

Olsen, D., and Stage, F. "Work Satisfaction and Stress in the First Three Years of an Academic Appointment." Paper presented at the annual meeting of the Association for the Study of Higher Education, Portland, Oregon, November 1990.

Peters, D. S., and Mayfield, J. R. "Are There Any Rewards for Teaching?" *Improving College and University Teaching,* 1982, *30* (3), 105–110.

Reynolds, A. "Making and Giving the Grade: Experiences of Beginning Professors at a Research University." Paper presented at the 72nd annual meeting of the American Edu-cational Research Association, New Orleans, Louisiana, April 1988.

Seldin, P. "Research Findings on Causes of Academic Stress." In P. Seldin (ed.), *Coping with Faculty Stress.* New Directions for Teaching and Learning, no. 29. San Francisco: Jossey-Bass, 1987.

Sorcinelli, M. D. "Faculty Careers: Personal, Institutional, and Societal Dimensions." Paper presented at the 69th annual meeting of the American Educational Research Association, Chicago, March 1985.

Sorcinelli, M. D. "Satisfactions and Concerns of New University Teachers." *To Improve the Academy,* 1988, *7,* 121–131.

Sorcinelli, M. D. "Chairs and the Development of New Faculty." *Department Advisor,* 1989, *5* (2), 1–4.

Sorcinelli, M. D., and Gregory, M. W. "Faculty Stress: The Tension Between Career Demands and Having It All." In P. Seldin (ed.), *Coping with Faculty Stress.* New Directions for Teaching and Learning, no. 29. San Francisco: Jossey-Bass, 1987.

Sorcinelli, M. D., and Near, J. "Relations Between Work and Life Away from Work Among University Faculty." *Journal of Higher Education,* 1989, *60* (1), 59–81.

Turner, J. L., and Boice, R. "Experiences of New Faculty." *Journal of Staff, Program, and Organizational Development,* 1989, *7* (2), 51–57.

Whitt, E. J. " 'Hit the Ground Running': Experiences of New Faculty in a School of Educa-tion." *Review of Higher Education,* 1991, *14* (2), 177–197.

Zanna, M. P., and Darley, J. M. (eds.). *The Compleat Academic: A Practical Guide for the Beginning Social Scientist.* New York: Random House, 1987.

MARY DEANE SORCINELLI is director of the Center for Teaching and associate ad-junct professor in the Division of Educational Policy and Administration, University of Massachusetts, Amherst.

Substantial orientation programs for faculty members who are new to an institution can provide major benefits for newcomers and their institutions. Moreover, these programs are neither difficult nor expensive to offer.

Orientation Programs for New Faculty

L. Dee Fink

Each year American institutions of higher education appoint thirty thousand to forty thousand new full-time faculty. These newcomers include experienced and senior faculty, but the vast majority are people who recently have received their doctoral degrees or the highest degrees available in their respective disciplines. In addition, although reliable estimates are hard to find, these same institutions also hire between eleven thousand and twenty thousand new people as part-time, adjunct faculty each year (Bowen and Schuster, 1986).

Most new members of the faculty are expected to start teaching classes right away. Those who are full-time are also expected to mount effective research programs and contribute to the service missions of their universities. Yet, it seems unrealistic to expect that new faculty members will know everything necessary to fulfill their responsibilities effectively. American graduate schools, in their more than a century of existence, have done a reasonably good job of ensuring that graduate students understand their disciplines and can undertake and complete small to medium size research projects. But graduate schools have not accepted any significant level of responsibility for the fuller preparation of those graduate students who intend to enter the academic profession (Fink, 1990).

Need for Additional Orientation

National and local studies have found that new faculty members face a variety of challenges as they set out to become fully functioning members of the faculty. The need for more support for teaching and scholarship from both colleagues and the institution seems paramount. In my national study of one hundred beginning college teachers, the respondents reported high levels of stress by the end of their first year (Fink, 1984). Part of this was due to heavy teaching loads. However, stress was not due to time taken to engage in creative teaching; most new faculty were lecturing almost all of the time, thereby teaching little more than "facts and principles." They were not, with few exceptions, challenging students to engage in critical thinking, using in- or out-of-class writing activities to deepen students' thinking abilities, or using small groups to encourage collaborative learning. They were not doing these things because no one had ever shown them how or told them that they could and should do more than lecture.

Although most of these new faculty had previously been teaching assistants, only one-half had ever had full responsibility for courses. And even for these, the "sink-or-swim" approach had taught them only how to survive; it had not shown them the possibilities of excellent college teaching. These same patterns were found in later studies conducted in individual institutions (Sorcinelli, 1988; Turner and Boice, 1989).

These studies answered another question: Are informal exchanges with more experienced colleagues able to address the professional orientation needs of new faculty? By and large, the answer is a resounding no. In my study, two-thirds of the new faculty indicated they had no or only limited "intellectual companionship" with their colleagues, that is, colleagues with whom they could discuss ideas and professional concerns (Fink, 1984, p. 49). Similarly, Sorcinelli (1988) found lack of collegial relations to be a major source of stress for new faculty, and Turner and Boice (1989, p. 55) found that relationships with colleagues were the "most salient and pervasive source of dissatisfaction." Boice (1990, this volume) provides evidence that a well-organized mentoring program can significantly change these relationships. But unless and until such programs become commonplace, colleague relationships will continue to be part of the problem, not part of the solution.

At the end of their first year, the participants in my study were asked to identify, in their own words, the single most important recommendation that they would make to institutions hiring new faculty members. The most frequent answer was the following: Provide better information at the start of the year (Fink, 1984, p. 107).

Since the variety of information needed—on roles, responsibilities, resources, and policies—is not yet being provided in graduate school or through informal contacts with more experienced fellow faculty members, the only way that new faculty will acquire these capabilities in any comprehensive way is for the employing institution to offer a substantial program of professional orientation for their new faculty members.

Five Programs for New Faculty

Part of the answer to the strong and obvious need for additional professional development lies in institutionally sponsored orientation programs for people with new academic appointments. Although many institutions have offered small evening or Saturday morning "welcoming" programs for a number of years, many universities have recently mounted more serious orientation programs. In this chapter, I describe select programs that well illustrate the diverse forms that these more substantial orientation programs can take.

Programs for new faculty can be offered in a variety of formats. One dimension of variation concerns their timing. Is the program held a week or two before the fall, or are meetings offered periodically throughout the fall semester or first year? A second dimension of variation concerns the content. Does the program focus primarily on preparation for effective teaching, or on institutional orientation, or does it try to address a wide range of professional development needs in teaching, research, and institutional operations? Third, is the program voluntary or mandatory? Fourth, who is the intended audience: full-time faculty members, part-time adjunct appointees, or both groups? Fifth, is the program centralized, with one program for all new faculty members in the university, or decentralized, with separate programs for new people in each college or department?

The five programs described here illustrate successful versions within each of these five dimensions of variation. The examples also illustrate how orientation programs can operate in different institutional settings. Three of the programs (University of Texas, University of Illinois, and University of Oklahoma) are in large state universities with major research expectations of the faculty; one (Southeast Missouri State University) is in a smaller regional university that is focused primarily on a teaching mission; and one (University College in the University of Maryland system) is a special institution for nonresidential, adult students. For readers who are interested in additional information, a contact person is listed for each program.

Presemester, Centralized. The University of Texas at Austin was one of the first universities to offer a presemester, centralized program. This program, sponsored by the Center for Teaching Effectiveness, began in 1980 and has been modified in a number of important ways over the years (Lewis, Svinicki, and Stice, 1985).

At first, the program had a five-day format (three full days and two half-days) and was offered the week before fall registration. All tenure track appointees who attended were paid a stipend of one week's salary, and topics focused primarily on teaching. In the mid 1980s, budget constraints forced a cessation of the stipend and a reduction in the length of the program to three full days. For other reasons, the content was broadened to include sessions that oriented new faculty members to the campus, to Austin, and to Texas and that introduced the various support services available to faculty and their students (for example, the Measurement and Evaluation Center, Learning Skills Center, and Dean of Students Office).

This program remains voluntary. In most years, the university hires

150 to 175 new faculty members. During the ten or so years that the program has been offered, about 40 percent of the total number of new faculty members each year attend. It is noteworthy that participation rates did not drop after the elimination of the stipends.

Although the program is organized by the Center for Teaching Effectiveness, most of the sessions are run by thirty-five to forty veteran faculty members. These colleagues have been quite willing to give of their time and expertise to help the newcomers.

The cost of the program before the budget cut was $30,000 to $40,000. Since 1985, the remaining direct costs have been approximately $2,500 per year for materials, coffee breaks, and the opening-day luncheon provided by the Office of the President.

In this highly successful program, only two significant problems have been encountered. First, there is uneven support from department chairs. Some strongly encourage new faculty to attend; others show less support. Second, some new faculty are still just moving in and are drawn away from the orientation by personal demands.

Contact person: Karron Lewis, Center for Teaching Effectiveness, Main Building 2200, University of Texas, Austin, TX 78712-1111. Phone: 512-471-1488.

Presemester, Mandatory. In 1986, Southeast Missouri State University, in Cape Girardeau, initiated a week-long teaching effectiveness workshop for all newly hired full-time faculty members (Renegar, Summary, Bonwell, and Eison, 1987). In this case, however, the initial planning committee made the recommendation, eventually approved by the Council of Deans, that the program be mandatory. This decision was based in part on a desire to communicate clearly, from the outset, that "the number one goal of the faculty" at this institution is teaching excellence, and in part on the belief that a stimulating and informative teaching effectiveness workshop can benefit all faculty. To "sweeten" the deal, the university agreed to give each participant a $250 honorarium for attending the workshop. The five main sections of the initial workshop focused on the tasks of designing course syllabi and writing behavioral objectives, teaching critical thinking, conducting discussions, lecturing skillfully, and constructing tests.

Although the initial attitude of the participants toward being required to attend was negative, the vast majority was "won over" by the end of the workshop and affirmed the value of the program in their evaluations. Nonetheless, the program directors solicited and attended to suggestions for change and improvement. As a result, several changes were made (Eison, 1989).

First, although the program directors decided to retain the mandatory status of the workshop, they prepared better preworkshop communications to counter negative preconceptions and create positive expectations. Second, they conducted a preprogram survey, not only to get information about the new faculty (for example, many of the participants in the first workshop had extensive prior teaching experience) but also to identify preferences among several possible workshop topics and to determine if the incoming faculty had areas of expertise that they would be willing to share. Third, new sessions were added pertaining to both the local community and the institution. Finally, they modified the time structure of the program to allow for more flexibility and free time. Thus, although the first day remains a mandatory all-day session, for the next four days only the morning sessions are required, and the afternoons are scheduled with optional activities (for example, a library tour and a presentation on student advising procedures). The cost is about $12,000 for a group of thirty-five participants, 75 percent of which is for the honoraria.

What have been the results thus far? In the words of the current director, "Responses have been overwhelmingly positive." Furthermore, attendance has been essentially 100 percent. Although there is still some initial skepticism and even resistance, the highly interactive character of the workshop and the visibility of the commitment to the premise that as professionals we can all learn from each other have led to nearly unanimous support. Additional evidence of the positive reputation of the program is that in 1991 two tenured faculty requested permission to attend the workshop.

Contact person: Charles Bonwell, Director, Center for Teaching and Learning, Southeast Missouri State University, Cape Girardeau, MO 63701. Phone: 314-651-2298.

During Semester, Decentralized. At the University of Illinois, in Urbana, the Division of Instructional Development (DID) within the Office of Instructional Resources has attempted to reach the relatively large number of new faculty, usually around two hundred each year, by working through individual colleges and departments to develop new faculty seminars. These efforts actually began around 1979 in the College of Veterinary Medicine but increased in size and number in the mid 1980s.

The "Dean's Seminar" is typically sponsored by an individual dean of a college and developed and implemented by the DID staff and a college-level committee. The seminars meet two to six times during the school year and deal with such topics as student feedback, facilitative instruction and critical thinking, lesson planning and organization, cognitive styles, cheating and discipline-specific topics. The first sessions may be designed for new faculty only; other sessions may include experienced as well as new faculty.

This program has the substantial advantage of carrying a dean's support in saying that "teaching matters in this college" and "here are some things you can learn about it." The obvious disadvantage is that the reach of the program is "hit and miss": Some deans offer the program in their colleges and others do not. Several of the major professional colleges (for example, Commerce and Business Administration, Engineering, and Agriculture) sponsor similar programs, but the largest college on campus, Liberal Arts and Sciences, has not yet become involved.

Contact person: Marne Helgesen, Head, Division of Instructional Development, 307 Engineering Hall, University of Illinois, Urbana, IL 61801. Phone: 217-333-3370.

During Semester, Centralized. At the University of Oklahoma, in Norman, the Instructional Development Program initiated a Professional Development Seminar for new faculty members in 1988. This program differs from the three preceding types of programs in two ways. First, the format of the program consists of a weekly seminar that meets throughout the first semester for lunch followed by the program. This extended format allows the content of the program to be presented in small "servings" that can be "digested" more easily and more fully before a "new meal" is served. It also allows the participants to form bonds and networks as a group since they meet fourteen different times during the first semester.

Second, the program has a broader scope than the other programs. The title and focus of the program is "professional development" rather than primarily "instructional development." Hence, the program includes sessions on (1) research, for example, how to find funding for and establish one's research program, (2) teaching, with sessions on such topics as innovative techniques and evaluation of one's own teaching, and (3) the resources and organization of the university.

During the four years that the program has been offered, approximately 75 percent of all new faculty members have registered for the seminar. The sign-up rate for incoming senior faculty, including new chairs, has been even higher than the rate of new assistant professors; presumably, the veterans know how useful such information is and are less inclined to try to adapt to a new university environment on their own.

Attendance generally starts high, averaging about 80 percent of those enrolled during the first third of the semester, and then levels off to an average of around 60 percent for the rest of the semester. Overall, 65 percent of the enrollees attend at least half of the fourteen sessions.

Most of the sessions are presented by either the directors of university offices (for example, library, computer center, research proposal services) or by veteran faculty members. As director of the Instructional Development Program, I run only three sessions on selected aspects of college teaching. The only expensive part of the program is the lunches, which constitute 90 percent of the total annual cost of $7,000.

We have made only two significant changes since starting the program. First, we shortened the program time from ninety minutes to seventy-five minutes. The original sessions ran a bit too long; the new length works well. Second, in 1990 we tried using "recent new faculty" to help that year's new faculty anticipate and cope with challenging experiences. For one session, we invited several third-year faculty to have lunch with us and then stay on as a panel to describe their own first-year experiences and answer questions. This session went very well.

Contact person: L. Dee Fink, Instructional Development Program, Carnegie 116, University of Oklahoma, Norman, OK 73019. Phone: 405-325-3521.

Adjunct Faculty. All four of the programs outlined above target full-time faculty. But most universities have a large number of part-time, adjunct faculty who are eager to learn more about effective teaching and how to function effectively within the university.

The University of Maryland, in College Park, consists of eleven institutions. One of these, University College, is distinctive in several ways: It is specifically for adult learners, generally off campus; it has the largest number of students of any institution in the Maryland system; and virtually all of its faculty are adjuncts, usually professionals in the Baltimore-Washington corridor. By definition, these faculty are not career academics. But their decision to teach, generally on an overload basis, means that they are attracted to teaching and see it as a valuable complement to their other professional activities. This interest in teaching, and the fact that University College hires 150 to 200 first-time adjuncts per year, creates a major need and opportunity for a strong orientation program.

University College has responded by sponsoring a one-evening, three-hour orientation program for this group. The program is repeated three times a year for successive groups of new faculty. A total of 115 people, 65 to 70 percent of all new adjuncts, attend one or another of these programs.

The intent of the program is to inform the newcomers about support services for faculty and students and to provide exciting ideas about quality teaching. The first goal is addressed by giving each participant a "survival kit" with materials on a large array of services and then reinforcing this information with a small number of presentations during the first half of the program. In pursuit of the second goal, the organizers try to model the Seven Principles of Good Practice for Undergraduate Education developed under the auspices of the American Association of Higher Education and the Education Commission of the States (Chickering and Gamson, 1991). This application of the Seven Principles entails several different teaching-learning activities: an icebreaker, a role play, a think-pair-share exercise, and a small group discussion on a two-page case study, "Bill Jasper's First Night of Class."

The cost of the program is low. Apart from the organizer's time, the direct cost is about $2,500 for all three offerings. For the total of around 115 participants each year, this constitutes a direct cost of just over $21 per faculty member.

Contact person: Barbara Millis, Assistant Dean, University of Maryland

University College, University Boulevard at Adelphi Road, College Park, MD 20742-1660. Phone: 301-985-7770.

Summary of Results and Costs

What can an institution expect in the way of benefits and costs if it decides to sponsor a substantial orientation program for new faculty members? Let me address this question first in terms of three aspects of the results and then in terms of the costs.

Attendance. What kind of participation rates can one expect from incoming faculty members? The answer depends on the kind of program offered. If the program is mandatory, as it is at Southeast Missouri State University, the sign-up and participation rates throughout the five-day period are essentially 100 percent. If the program is voluntary but centralized, as at the University of Oklahoma and University of Texas, the attendance is likely to be around 50 percent of the total group of new faculty members. If the program is decentralized, as at the University of Illinois, the "reach" of the program will vary widely and depend on the degree of cooperation from individual deans and chairs, but the participation rate is likely to be in the 20 to 40 percent range. The kind of program chosen should obviously be based on an intent to reach as many people as possible. But local political factors also need to be considered, such as whether a mandatory or centralized program is politically feasible.

Value for Individual Faculty Members. Given the experience of several programs to date, what are the benefits that can reasonably be expected for the individual faculty members? First, they learn how to approach basic professional responsibilities more systematically and with a better information base. In terms of teaching responsibilities, almost all of the program directors have seen a significant increase in the number of faculty members who know about and use active learning strategies such as in-class writing and small groups. In those orientation programs that include sessions on research activities, faculty members have been submitting grant proposals at a high rate, in part because they know about the services available at the institution to support this activity. Second, the faculty members establish lasting contacts with other faculty members around campus. Life for new people in large organizations can be lonely and isolated. But contacts with colleagues, both other new colleagues and more experienced ones, can start a networking process that increases a faculty member's personal, social, and professional vitality. Finally, assuming the people who make presentations are honest and candid, newcomers can quickly get a sense of the real values of the institutions, the current directions in which the college or university is heading, and its priorities.

Overall, these benefits essentially mean that a substantial orientation program constitutes, in the words of one participant, a "head start" for new faculty. They know "where" they are, they know with whom they are working, and they know the preferred operating procedures. As a result, they generally feel less anxious, which in turn allows them to perform their professional activities more effectively and more creatively. Most people seem to enjoy and prefer this kind of working situation.

Value for the Institution. Even apart from what these programs can and do accomplish for individual faculty members, the institutions realize a number of important organizational benefits. First, these types of programs shorten the learning time needed for newcomers to become fully functioning members of the organization. All organizations have the problem of trying to get new people working "up to speed" as soon as possible. Effective orientation programs can significantly shorten this learning time.

Second, several program directors have noted that these programs seem to increase the ability of faculty members to identify with the whole college or university. This identification is generally considered a valuable counterbalance to the strong tendency in American higher education for academics, especially graduate students and new faculty, to identify almost completely with their respective disciplines or departments. This latter kind of identification is valid and worthy, but it is helpful to the campus community when these allegiances are balanced by positive associations with the institution as a whole.

Third, to the degree that the program includes sessions on institutional orientation as well as on instructional improvement, the institution can operate more efficiently when the faculty know the preferred operating procedures and the reasons for these procedures. As word about the University of Oklahoma program spread throughout the university community, several offices asked to join the program so that they could systematically educate the faculty about how to use their services.

Fourth, these programs can be very effective tools for faculty recruitment and retention. The programs are generally perceived by candidates for faculty positions as evidence of real institutional concern and support for faculty welfare and professional development. Similarly, once on board, people who have been able to learn quickly what they need to know to be fully functioning faculty members, and who feel supported in that effort, are likely to be happier, to feel more "at home," and to opt to stay when given a chance to leave.

Costs. Like all programs, a good orientation program for new faculty incurs costs, and an institution needs to project these costs in order to decide whether the benefits justify the expense in terms of both time and money.

How much time does a good program require? The actual total program times at three of the institutions described above are very similar: about three days. At Texas, these are three continuous full days; at Southeast Missouri State, the time is one full-day and four half-days; at Oklahoma, there are fourteen sessions, each lasting seventy-five minutes.

The other significant time cost is the time that it takes the program organizer to plan, conduct, evaluate, and do the follow-up work associated with a good program. The best estimate of program directors is that the work ratio is 5:1, that is, five days of administrative work for each day of program presentation. So, for example, a three-day program would require fifteen days of associated work, and if the organizer has a salary of approximately $40,000 per year (close to the national average of faculty salaries), the organizer's time costs in days translate to nearly $2,500.

The other major type of cost is financial. Money is needed to cover the cost of materials and possibly honoraria, meals, and rooms. However, the amount of financial support needed varies considerably from program to program, depending on whether honoraria are given, whether meals are provided, and whether the program has to pay for rooms.

Are the benefits worth the likely costs? In my view the answer is clearly yes. To take the Oklahoma program as an example, if the time of the program organizer is included, the total annual cost is around $10,000, which may appear substantial. Analyzed in terms of cost per participating faculty member, however, the cost is approximately $250. Assuming the benefit of the program lasts only two years (a very conservative estimate), the total financial cost per faculty member represents less than 0.5 percent of a new faculty member's salary for two years. This cost is an extraordinarily small investment in faculty development with the potential for realizing several kinds of major benefits!

Conclusions and Recommendations

Institutions that are serious about the professional development of their faculty must at the very least give consideration to the value of having strong orientation programs for new faculty members at their campuses. The potential benefits are quite high; the costs, as an investment in the professional competence of the faculty, are relatively low; and there are several models from which to choose in order to adapt to local conditions.

For those who decide to establish this kind of program, several recommendations bear consideration. First, the scope of the program should be broad. That is, it should include an orientation to the institution as well as sessions on improving teaching and—if appropriate—sessions on establishing a research program. There are important lessons to be learned about each of these activities.

Second, all sessions in the program should "practice what is preached" by being models of good teaching. Given all of the information that needs to be delivered, it is very easy to fall into the traditional presentational mode. Resist the temptation. The best and liveliest sessions are those that have deliberately provided for active learning by participants, such as writing and small group discussion.

Third, the program should be designed to create opportunities for the participants to interact with each other as much as possible. The goal of helping new faculty establish contacts for future networking is one of the more important aspects of the program.

Fourth, program directors should take care not to overload the participants. All of the research on new faculty members indicates that they have a mountain of responsibilities and are under a lot of stress. Hence, whichever time format is used, directors need to find ways to "create time and space" so the participants can digest the ideas encountered in the program without putting off other responsibilities for too long a time.

To conclude, I share an observation from a survey of faculty development specialists a few years ago about programs for new faculty members (Eison and Hill, 1990). When asked to provide any final advice to campuses interested in creating a program for newly hired faculty, one respondent said simply, "Do it. . . . It's fun, easy, not expensive, and builds community plus teaching effectiveness." Good advice.

References

Boice, R. "Mentoring New Faculty: A Program for Implementation." *Journal of Staff, Program, and Organization Development,* 1990, *8* (3), 143–160.

Bowen, H. R., and Schuster, J. H. *American Professors: A National Resource Imperiled.* New York: Oxford University Press, 1986.

Chickering, A. W., and Gamson, Z. F. (eds.). *Applying the Seven Principles of Good Practice for Undergraduate Education.* New Directions for Teaching and Learning, no. 47. San Francisco: Jossey-Bass, 1991.

Eison, J. A. "Mandatory Teaching Effectiveness Workshops for New Faculty: What a Difference Three Years Make." *Journal of Staff, Program, and Organization Development,* 1989, 7 (2), 59–66.

Eison, J. A., and Hill, H. H. "Creating Workshops for New Faculty." *Journal of Staff, Program, and Organization Development,* 1990, 8 (4), 223–234.

Fink, L. D. (ed.). *The First Year of College Teaching.* New Directions for Teaching and Learning, no. 17. San Francisco: Jossey-Bass, 1984.

Fink, L. D. "New Faculty Members: The Professoriate of Tomorrow." *Journal of Staff, Program, and Organization Development,* 1990, 8 (4), 235–245.

Lewis, K. G., Svinicki, M. D., and Stice, J. E. "Filling the Gap: Introducing New Faculty to the Basics of Teaching." *Journal of Staff, Program, and Organization Development,* 1985, *3* (1), 16–31.

Renegar, S., Summary, B., Bonwell, C., and Eison, J. "Mandatory Teaching Effective Workshops for New Faculty: Lessons Learned the Hard Way." *Journal of Staff, Program, and Organization Development,* 1987, 5 (3), 114–118.

Sorcinelli, M. D. "Satisfactions and Concerns of New University Teachers." *To Improve the Academy,* 1988, 7, 121–131.

Turner, J. L., and Boice, R. "Experiences of New Faculty." *Journal of Staff, Program, and Organization Development,* 1989, 7 (2), 51–57.

L. DEE FINK is director of the Instructional Development Program at the University of Oklahoma, Norman.

Studies of mentoring for new faculty reveal principles for its maximization, including a more directive and collective format for mentors.

Lessons Learned About Mentoring

Robert Boice

In a sense, we know a lot about mentoring. It is akin to parenting. It is as old as apprenticeship, coaching, and teaching. Yet, we are only beginning to learn the specifics of how best to mentor new faculty. Recent reviews of the literature of mentoring show an emphasis on other kinds of pairings, primarily in graduate schools or in business settings (Lavery, Boice, Thompson, and Turner, 1989). What may be most obvious about mentoring for new faculty is its unfamiliarity as a subject of inquiry (Boice, 1990; Sands, Parson, and Duane, 1991).

What hinders knowledge about mentoring? Part of the problem may be that mentoring often occurs in a gradual, unsystematic fashion, making it hard to study. And part of the enigma may owe to concerns about its possible status as a mere fad in faculty development (Weimer, 1990). We have been, until now, ambivalent about mentoring. Consider that heretofore the only proven benefits of social networks in professorial careers have accrued to scholarly productivity, not to teaching (Creswell, 1985).

Despite these obstacles, though mentoring is becoming a more popular part of plans and programs for new faculty. As we work harder to attract and retain the best people to professorial careers, we can no longer afford to ignore potential supports that can make a traditionally forbidding career seem more survivable (Boice, 1992; Bowen and Schuster, 1986; Schuster, 1990).

This chapter provides an overview of recent research on mentoring for new faculty and makes two related points. First, recent studies of mentor-mentee pairs suggest practical guidelines for maximizing the mentoring experience. Second, close examination of traditional mentoring pairs, even those operating in exemplary fashion, suggests a shortcoming of traditional

New Directions for Teaching and Learning, no. 50, Summer 1992 ©Jossey-Bass Publishers mentoring formats. Usual pairs of mentors and new faculty may work in too passive a fashion to help many new faculty, especially minorities, thrive in professorial careers. Thus, we face a frustration in getting to know mentoring as a tool for supporting new faculty: Just as we begin to understand its mechanisms, we may need to change them.

A Study of Traditional Mentoring Pairs

Elsewhere, in laborious detail, I described a multiyear project on mentoring at a large comprehensive university (Boice, 1990). Briefly, that federally funded project had two stages. In the first, my colleague Jimmie L. Turner and I surveyed the spontaneous occurrence of mentoring on campus during 1985–1986. Among the forty to sixty new faculty hired each year on tenure-track positions, only a handful participated in mentoring of any significant sort. But, those who had it clearly fared better than did the majority without it.

Given the usual complaints of these and similar new faculty about social isolation and intellectual understimulation, the situation seemed ripe for a systematic program for mentoring. Indeed, new faculty routinely gave high ratings in response to questions about their desire for mentoring.

The second stage of the project consisted of establishing twenty-five mentoring pairs for sustained study for at least an academic year of regular weekly meetings and other activities. Roughly one-half were what we termed *traditional mentoring pairs:* mentors and mentees essentially picked each other, mentors were older than mentees, and pairs were often from within the same departments. The procedure for forming the other pairs was dictated by practicalities. Many new faculty in the study were hired into departments without obvious or willing mentors among their more senior colleagues. So, some new hires were paired with mentors from other departments (who, like more traditional mentors, were selected for participation on the basis of demonstrated excellence and balance as teachers and researchers).

A variety of measures, including self-ratings by pair members and my own direct observations of pairs in action, indicated that all but a few of these pairs were highly successful. As a rule, mentoring was associated with more rapid socialization to campus and with improved student ratings of teaching compared to nonmentored peers. As a rule, both mentors and mentees listed a wealth of benefits for having participated in what initially seemed a time-consuming project. Overall, intensive study of the twenty-five mentoring pairs suggested five general outcomes that may have value to other campuses:

Arbitrarily Paired Mentors and Mentees Worked as Well as Traditional Pairs. Initially, arbitrarily paired mentors and mentees were highly skeptical. "How," each routinely asked, "am I supposed to get close to someone like him [her]? I probably would have picked someone different." Soon, though, arbitrarily matched pairs minimized this problem. They discovered that the kinds of coping skills essential to survival were the same for all new faculty regardless of department. Pairs mixed across genders and ethnicities fared as well as unmixed pairs.

One feature seemed to make these arbitrary pairs slightly more successful in final ratings. Traditional pairs, who picked each other, often had prior histories of friendships. When one of them assumed the role of mentor, strife ensued. Mentees in these pairs resented the sudden change of status from supposed equals to unequals, especially when advice was tantamount to pressure to get at delayed tasks. These previously friendly pairs, incidentally, provided the only confirmations of a fear that bothered all mentors initially—the fear of being perceived as presumptuous in claiming the role of mentor.

The point of this finding is so simple that it can easily be missed. One of the seemingly most daunting tasks of setting up mentoring projects, one where the literature on mentoring provides little concrete help, is forming effective pairs of mentors and mentees. This study suggests that the process of meeting regularly in supportive fashion is more important than the personal characteristics of the pair members. That is, almost any new faculty can benefit from mentoring, regardless of the similarity or dissimilarity of the qualified colleague sharing his or her professorial experience and support.

Mentors from Same and Different Departments Worked at Least as Well. Here too, pairs began with doubts, whether paired voluntarily or arbitrarily. "How," each wondered, "can someone from a different department, or even school, begin to understand the special needs of my discipline or the special politics of my department?" I wondered too.

But this problem was soon mastered. Pairs, often with advice from other pairs, learned to send mentors to discuss departmental expectations for their mentees with the departmental chairpeople and retention-tenure committees. And, just as quickly, these pairs found that the kinds of coping skills most essential to thriving on a new campus were not specific to disciplines. The essence of good mentoring, according to almost all pairs, was socioemotional support.

In the final analysis, two characteristics of these cross-departmental mentor-mentee pairs seemed to contribute to their slightly greater success compared to more traditional mentoring pairs. The first was their mutual effort to learn about the cultures of each other's departments. The other was a readier openness of mentees with mentors from different departments. A common concern of the mentees with mentors from their own departments was that self-disclosures of failings might be held against them in retention-tenure decisions. Mentees with close colleagues as mentors acted conservatively and defensively at times.

Frequent Nudges to Meet Regularly Helped Ensure Pair Bonds. Because I was intent on studying the mentoring experience in progress, I did something that I might not otherwise have done. I had pairs keep checklists, journals of what happened during weekly mentoring meetings, and ratings of each other's involvement, helpfulness, and other presumed qualities of effective mentoring. Then, to ensure that data were being collected, I contacted pairs weekly or biweekly in person or by telephone to collect their notes and ratings and make my own.

As a result, of this simple action of making regular contacts, more was accomplished than the collection of fascinating information about the progress of mentoring pairs. Initially, pair members complained that the contacts were a nuisance. Eventually, though, the pairs came to value them. My contacts came to be seen as chances to reflect on a valued experience. Moreover, everyone noted, my contacts had acted as prods to keep pairs meeting when mentees and mentors had felt too busy to meet. Without my reminders that they should meet at least weekly for brief exchanges, they said, they would surely have stopped meeting. This prodding, more than anything else, helped ensure the bonds and habits of meeting regularly that contributed to the success of their pairs.

Left to Themselves, Most Mentoring Pairs Displayed Disappointingly Narrow Styles. Even where mentors had considerable seasoning at mentoring, they typically worked with mentees on a limited range of topics. Some mentors focused almost exclusively on preparing retention-tenure materials, others on coaching for writing productivity. Not until they were in monthly meetings where all mentoring pairs shared experiences did most pairs expand their horizons. Then, once freed from whatever invisible bounds had been in effect, pairs began trying creative activities (such as visits to the special collections room of the library, the faculty computer laboratory, and the weight room in the gymnasium). Perhaps because participants were accustomed to professorial mentoring that occurs in offices with students, mentors and mentees had not thought of alternatives in location or content. Once this broadening of perspectives began, pair members reported more enjoyment of mentoring and of their partners.

Mentors Assumed the Role of Interventionist with Reluctance. Despite the bonding and positive results, mentors resisted my attempts to move them beyond relatively passive roles of listening and giving occasional advice. If, for example, mentees were failing as teachers, mentors would wait for them to ask for help. And, when help was requested, it usually came in terms of vague admonitions to reduce the level of difficulty of course materials or to induce more active student involvement in classes. While such advice helped reassure mentees, it rarely translated into obviously improved teaching.

When I asked mentors about their reasons for not doing more, their answers were uniform and interesting: For one thing, they typically began, they did not want to impose themselves on mentees; faculty, even novices, should be autonomous in their classrooms. For another, they were not sure that teaching could be taught except by experience; they themselves had learned without help beyond occasional bits of advice. And, to complete the list, they noted that if mentoring required more than socioemotional support, they might decline to do it. They suspected that they had no time or inclination to do more.

Only when I structured the task of coaching mentees at teaching did mentors get more involved. They agreed, once involved, that brief visits to mentees' classes and subsequent feedback on a brief checklist could be managed in a constructive fashion. And they found that the practice of bringing their mentees to their own classes, wherein a brief, specific strategy for teaching was modeled for the mentees' benefit, was both helpful and reasonable. Much like the initial narrowness in perspective of mentoring pairs described above, the lack of proactiveness owed more to uncertainty about how to proceed than to conscious resistance.

General Lesson. Taken together, these five guidelines suggest a general principle for maximizing the usefulness of mentoring programs: Mentoring pairs may need considerable mentoring, including prods, directives, and chances to show off successes. But as I brought those guidelines to another mentoring project at my new campus, I began to notice a dark side to that general lesson. As we usually see it practiced, mentoring for new faculty is surprisingly ineffective. Without some kind of program such as the one just described, pairs tend to stop meeting (no matter how well intentioned), to work in narrow fashion, and even to let mentees fail for lack of intervention.

But that is not all. Once my presence as a recruiter and prodder of pair members was gone from the project, the mentees most likely to become uninvolved were minorities. Traditional mentoring is passive in terms of self-initiative for new faculty in general, and for the new recruits that we most need to nurture and retain in particular. To counter this inertia, I have begun to experiment with nontraditional mentoring for minority new faculty. While the results are only preliminary, they suggest a way of improving on traditional mentor-mentee pairings for new faculty.

Nontraditional Mentoring

The logic in looking for alternative approaches to mentoring new faculty goes beyond the mixed results just reviewed. Clearly, mentoring based on the model of a dissertation adviser and graduate student is too constraining for new hires. In finishing our dissertations, it may have made sense to model our efforts after an individual's approach to research. Heaven knows that even for such a limited purpose, doctoral mentoring has a strikingly poor track record; my own interviews with new faculty commonly reveal bitterness and mistreatment connected to doctoral advisers. Moreover, some observers of academe estimate that one-half of the graduate students who complete their coursework and qualifying exams never finish their dissertations (D. Sternberg, 1981).

When new colleagues and come to campus, the paradigm of aligning each of them with a single individual, with the single goal of carrying out a specific research program, is even less appropriate. New faculty need to bond with groups, on and off campus, with departments and campuses, with administrators, and with students. They must, to state the matter simply, please more than one person.

Recently, I undertook a study of new faculty who found quick success as teachers and as productive researchers and scholars (Boice, 1991). Three characteristics of these "quick starters" are relevant here: First, they constitute a small minority, perhaps of no more than 10 to 15 percent of new faculty at large campuses. Second, they are, so far, almost exclusively white and male. And, third, they are unique in seeking out social supports and advice from a variety of colleagues, especially those in the position to make decisions about their retention and tenure. While quick starters do not necessarily ingratiate themselves with influential colleagues, they do get constant feedback about whether their activities are sufficient in quantity and quality.

In my own studies of new faculty who appear likely to fail in professorial careers, the opposite pattern emerged. These are people, like the marginal and minority faculty studied elsewhere (Exum, Menges, Watkins, and Berglund, 1984), who not only are highly distressed over their social isolation but also show confusion about what is expected of them. Too often, they learn about norms and expectations only in retention or tenure reports, long after corrections would help.

What slower starters needed, I imagined, was something similar to what had been used more than a decade ago in studies of reengaging middle-aged, disillusioned faculty. They too needed clear directives, incentives, and social supports. The key element in that earlier work was a form of contracting that I came to call *cataloguing*.

Cataloguing. To ensure its widespread adoption among new faculty who suppose themselves too busy for most additional activities, the technique of cataloguing has to be brief but effective. In essence, new faculty are asked to compile and continually revise catalogues of succinct, readable descriptions of past activities, current activities, and planned activities. Because these three- to seven-page catalogues are easiest to conceptualize in relation to writing projects, I encourage new faculty to begin in that domain. Thus, each manuscript already published, in press, or in progress is described in a paragraph. And, in like fashion, planned manuscripts are described with details about their messages and significance, about their concordance with the individual's research and scholarly program in general, and about their intended outlets for publication.

Similar sets of descriptions make up catalogues for other vital activities such as teaching, collegial networking, and service. Although modest amounts of coaching and modeling are helpful in setting up catalogues, new faculty, in my experience, master this task rather effortlessly (Boice, 1992).

As described so far, cataloguing is anything but unusual. We already know of kindred devices such as portfolios that help gain untenured faculty credit for accomplishments beyond publication lists. And we can, those of us who know ourselves and our colleagues all too well, easily envision cataloguing as something that starts with enthusiasm and fades when new hires become immersed in their busy work weeks. What makes cataloguing work is its linkage to a special kind of mentoring for new faculty: group mentoring.

Committees as Mentors. Again, the task of the mentors is kept brief but effective. I ask the departments modeling this group mentoring to assign as mentors the same individuals who will make retention-tenure decisions for a new hire down the road. I also ask that the committee mentoring and the cataloguing be initiated as early as possible. Indeed, the first occasion where the group of mentors gives feedback about how much is enough and whether plans and topics are on track is when the potential mentee comes to campus as a job candidate.

Thus, the candidate, who submits a brief catalogue for teaching and for writing preliminary to his or her visit, gets the first round of feedback about what is expected early in the process of being a new faculty member. Even then, the occasion is set to accomplish three other facets of the mentoring that are essential in the long run. First, every attempt is made to avoid surprises (on both sides) about what is required and expected. Second, opportunities for soliciting and offering support and advice are made apparent (for example, how to plan and carry out a reasonable set of goals). Here, more than in traditional mentoring, opportunities for help are almost unavoidable. Third, the interaction gives faculty prospects a sense of a campus prepared to provide supports.

In my observations so far of eight minority faculty who are already engaged in cataloguing and group mentoring, these initial and subsequent meetings have a predictable set of characteristics:

1. New faculty and mentors alike claim immediate benefits of analyzing past, ongoing, and planned accomplishments. The task is especially illuminating for activities not ordinarily specified in written fashion such as teaching (where learning goals and designs for improving may otherwise have been vague or absent) and social networking (where little attention is typically paid to arranging and carrying out beneficial contacts for research and teaching).

2. New faculty express public relief at knowing what is expected and at being able to negotiate compromises in expectations. They also report far less private worrying about the fairness of the evaluation procedure

leading to retention or tenure decisions than do new minority faculty not in the program.

3. Mentoring committees and mentees report surprise at how little time the catalogue feedback sessions take. In general, after the initial meetings, monthly group meetings (always with the mentee in attendance) take about thirty minutes. Other interactions, usually between mentees and individual mentors, typically consist of delivery of revised or annotated catalogues, clarification of the nature of plans and expectations, and advice about how goals can be met. It is, in my experience, common for these mentors and mentees to misunderstand each other at the outset. Eventually, the communication of expectations, plans, and supports becomes more efficient.

4. Mentoring committees and their mentees say that the two best aspects of this project are (1) the unprecedented feelings of collegiality, of belonging, and of caring and (2) the eventual painlessness of the evaluations. Over time, mentoring groups suppose, the expectations and progress toward goals become so clear that the mentees will know the retention-tenure decision in advance.

5. The mentoring committees conclude that two factors make the difference in nurturing their minority mentees: One, already mentioned, is the clarification of expectations and of what are in fact reasonable accomplishments for the new colleagues under constant scrutiny. The other is that group members, once they become invested in their mentees, stimulate each other to provide active supports for them. Examples recorded so far include brief ventures in coteaching and in collaborative writing with mentees.

Despite these promising beginnings, questions remain. What, for instance, will keep cataloguing groups on a regular schedule of meetings? The answer in part may be that the mentoring committees expect to carry their commitments for at least as long as decisions remain to be made. While they might not otherwise meet and evaluate in ongoing fashion, these committees report intentions to continue functioning, at least biannually, until they complete their goals. Another part of the answer is that cataloguing groups seem to enjoy themselves. A final part of the answer may be that high-level administrators will give more authorization and funding to a project that focuses on supporting new minority faculty than to most faculty development programs.

Another question that arises when I discuss cataloguing groups with others on my own campus and elsewhere is why I limit the process to new minority faculty. My answer is that I began the project with the new faculty most in need of support and most likely to end up isolated and unhappy on campus. Next, I add an optimistic note. I expect that departments with cataloguing groups, when they acknowledge their successes, will help me institute cataloguing for all of their new faculty.

Finally, fellow practitioners often ask me to ground my ideas in more familiar approaches to faculty development. As a result, I have found a way to embed cataloguing in a simple composite theory formed from already successful approaches to student and faculty development. The abbreviated name of the theory is IRSS: *I*nvolvement, *R*egimen, *S*olving the right problem, and *S*ocial networking.

IRSS Theory and Cataloguing Groups. The kinds of things that new faculty must master first for success in academic careers are of the most basic sort, so elementary that we ordinarily overlook them. The first of the four IRSS factors is the simplest and the most firmly established.

Involvement. The notion comes from student development and Astin's (1985) theory of involvement. Briefly, he found that students who immerse themselves in campus life, in activities and social networks, and who develop a sense of belonging fare better and stay longer. The same rule undoubtedly applies to new faculty. Cataloguing helps ensure that new-comers get involved—in supportive and communicative networks with influential faculty, in campus activities, and in developing a sense of trust in the campus.

Regimen. Cataloguing, put simply, is a matter of staying on schedule and of staying with the task of mentoring. This suspiciously behavioral notion of productivity by way of brief, daily sessions has roots in my work with new faculty who procrastinate (Boice, 1989).

Solving the Right Problem. This notion comes from composition teachers and from Flower's (1990) studies showing that students who fail as writers typically do so because they try to solve the wrong problems. She concludes that they can learn to write when they solve useful problems such as writing for the appropriate audience.

Here again, the rule applies to new faculty. Many of them try to solve problems such as finding big blocks of undisrupted time for writing and lecture preparation. Instead, the evidence (Boice, 1989) is that they do better when they solve the problem of time management by making tasks such as writing fit into the brief openings of already busy days. Cataloguing groups encourage accurate task representations by constantly keeping their mentees on the right tasks. With new minority faculty, for example, this assistance often takes the form of discouraging their overinvolvement in committees.

This third factor in the IRSS theory, like the other three factors, also has roots in recent insights about why students fail. Poor students do not know how to talk (or how not to talk) in class, how to apportion their time for studying, or how to study for tests (Sternberg, Okagaki, and Jackson, 1990). R. Sternberg's (1988) theoretical interpretation of these failures is that schools traditionally tend to ignore the teaching of tacit knowledge. While tacit knowledge is typically untaught, it is essential to thriving in academe.

Tacit knowledge is also critical to new faculty. They, like students, need to learn how to manage themselves, others, and tasks in order to thrive in academe. This need to learn subtle things may account for the enduring popularity of mentoring. Cataloguing provides the added measure of coaching from several mentors, all of whom are committed to regular interactions with mentees.

Social Networking. In a sense, this final IRSS theory component is preempted by what we have already covered here. Clearly, new faculty who find strong social networks have better chances of survival and success. But the theory behind this notion goes further. It says that those faculty who fare best strike a balance between teaching, scholarship, and collegial outreach. Thus, social networking, to be effective, occupies as much time as moderate investments in teaching preparation and in research and scholarship (Creswell, 1985).

What has balance got to do with cataloguing? In fact, the connection is tenuous so far. In my experience, the hardest thing to impart to new faculty, or to get cataloguing groups to induce in an effective way, is balance. Yet, it is this single component of adjusting to life as a new faculty member that the quick starters cite as pivotal in their successes (Boice, 1992). I continue to struggle with this dilemma, just one in the never-ending series of challenges that help keep faculty development in the realm of fun.

References

Astin, A. W. *Achieving Educational Excellence: A Critical Assessment of Priorities and Practices in Higher Education.* San Francisco: Jossey-Bass, 1985.

Boice, R. "Procrastination, Busyness, and Bingeing." *Behaviour Research and Therapy,* 1989, 27, 605–611.

Boice, R. "Mentoring New Faculty: A Program for Implementation." *Journal of Staff, Program, and Organization Development,* 1990, 8 (3), 143–160.

Boice, R. "Quick Starters." In M. Theall (ed.), *Improving the Practice of Teaching Development.* New Directions in Teaching and Learning, no. 48. San Francisco: Jossey-Bass, 1991.

Boice, R. *The New Faculty Member.* San Francisco: Jossey-Bass, 1992.

Bowen, J. R., and Schuster, J. H. *American Professors: A National Resource Imperiled.* New York: Oxford University Press, 1986.

Creswell, J. W. *Faculty Research Performance: Lessons from the Sciences and the Social Sciences.* ASHE-ERIC Higher Education Reports, no. 4. Washington, D.C.: Association for the Study of Higher Education, 1985.

Exum, W. M., Menges, R. J., Watkins, B., and Berglund, P. "Making It at the Top: Women and Minority Faculty in the Academic Labor Market." *American Behavioral Scientist,* 1984, 27, 301–324.

Flower, L. "The Role of Task Representation in Reading-to-Write." In L. Flower, V. Stein, J. Ackerman, M. J. Kantz, K. McCormick, and W. C. Peck (eds.), *Reading-to-Write.* New York: Oxford University Press, 1990.

Lavery, P. T., Boice, R., Thompson, R. W., and Turner, J. L. "An Annotated Bibliography of Mentoring for New Faculty." *Journal of Staff, Program, and Organization Development,* 1989, 7, 39–46.

Sands, R., Parson, L. A., and Duane, J. "Faculty Mentoring Faculty in a Public University." *Journal of Higher Education,* 1991, 62 (2), 174–193.

Schuster, J. H. Address delivered at the conference of the Professional and Organizational Development Network in Higher Education, Lake Tahoe, Nevada, November 2, 1990.

Sternberg, D. *How to Complete and Survive a Doctoral Dissertation.* New York: St. Martin's Press, 1981.

Sternberg, R. J. *The Triarchic Mind.* New York: Penguin, 1988.

Sternberg, R. J., Okagaki, L., and Jackson, A. S. "Practical Intelligence for Success in School." *Educational Leadership,* Sept. 1990, pp. 35–39.

Weimer, M. *Improving College Teaching: Strategies for Developing Instructional Effectiveness.* San Francisco: Jossey-Bass, 1990.

ROBERT BOICE is professor of psychology and director of the Faculty Instructional Support Office at the State University of New York, Stony Brook.

Those who fail to establish effective habits of research and writing early in their careers probably never will.

Improving Junior Faculty Scholarship

Donald K. Jarvis

The term *faculty development* has been narrowed in many academic communities to denote only the improvement of teaching. Few would deny that teaching requires more emphasis than it received in the 1970s and 1980s, but neglect of the development of faculty scholarship is counterproductive for academia, for the professor, and for development programs. Because professors' formal and informal incentives include discovery of new knowledge as well as its dissemination, development programs that include improvement of scholarship skills have more prestige, interest, and long-term value than do those restricted to teaching alone. In other words, most professors love teaching, but research provides clout. Developers have to pay attention to that fact of academic life.

While it could be argued that research is the one thing that graduate schools consistently prepare their students to do, in-service programs to enhance junior faculty scholarship are still needed. A young academic leaves graduate school and its relatively structured contact with peers and teachers for a relatively lonely struggle with pressing new demands at the first job: new classes, advising of students, a new home, and perhaps a dissertation to complete. For many, these urgent everyday tasks displace the important but less pressing responsibilities of scholarship. Because such choices soon become habits, professors' first employment influences their whole careers much more than does graduate training, and those who fail to establish effective habits of research and writing early in their careers probably never will (Creswell, 1985). Many American academic leaders discovered this fact between 1970 and 1985 when they tried to pressure nonpublishing senior faculty members to begin publishing late in their careers: The most notable result of this push to research and write was widespread alienation of nonpublishing senior professors (Bowen and Schuster, 1986).

A second argument for establishing a research improvement program for junior professors is that university-level research in the United States annually costs around $9.6 billion, $2.3 billion of which is provided by the universities themselves ("Campus Research," 1985). Some fraction of those huge sums should be spent on helping young researchers get off to a correct start.

Effective Design of Junior Faculty Development Programs

The recommendations in this chapter are derived from my recent studies of junior faculty development programs in the United States, interviews with over one hundred prominent American professors, and reviews of the general fields of personnel and faculty development (Jarvis, 1991). This project concerned a broad range of junior faculty issues, but the present chapter focuses on the development of research skills.

Administrative Support. Before delving into the specifics of how to develop research expertise, we should review a few general principles. The first principle of faculty development—as with any continuing interdisciplinary program—is to establish firm administrative support. Many good projects can be started from the grass roots, but public support from institutional leaders is usually necessary. This support includes a firm and well-publicized agreement on the goals of the developmental program and their value to the institution, modest funding, appointment of faculty leaders to manage the program, and provision of meeting space, office space, and staff support.

Good Management. The second principle of faculty development is good management. Siegel (1980, p. 137) concluded that "program management was far more important to the success of faculty development projects than was planning and preparation, since 'the road to Hell is paved with good intentions.'" He found that effective programs had a clearly structured decision-making unit that not only made the plans but followed through on their execution. Successful management groups clearly specified their program objectives and evaluation criteria from the outset, were flexible in their approaches, and were skilled at publicizing the program's existence, its relation to the institutional reward structure, the terms of participation, and the successes or failures of ongoing projects.

Orientation Toward the Future. An orientation toward the future is vital to faculty development. Faculty members must be helped to make long-range plans, to set specific goals, and to believe that their efforts will be rewarded. This future orientation is especially important for research, which frequently requires extensive planning to arrange schedules, funding applications, equipment, travel, and replacements. Department chairs should at least annually interview junior professors about their progress and plans for the future, rewarding small successes and avoiding excessive focus on past failures.

Collegiality. Perhaps the most important single factor in faculty development is the concept of collegiality, what historian Page Smith calls "the pursuit of truth in the company of friends." For scientific research, personal contacts with active colleagues on and off campus appear to be more important than printed matter and other impersonal communications (Creswell, 1985). Nobel-quality research is more often collaborative than individual, and accounts of great centers of scientific creativity often "note the presence of intensive interaction and competition" (Zuckerman, 1977, p. 172). Judging from the extensive study that I made of prominent American professors, contact with colleagues also stimulates research in the humanities (Jarvis, 1991). Conversely, when Boice (1973) studied nonpublishing professors, he found a high correlation between social isolation and noninvolvement in publication.

Writers on faculty development unanimously agree that collegiality is central to any successful development program for professors. Development of collegiality is a central goal in all of the best-known interinstitutional programs for junior faculty development, including those conducted by the Lilly Endowment, the Bush Foundation, the Central Pennsylvania Consortium, and the Great Lakes College Association (GLCA) (Jarvis, 1991). Common elaborations of this theme included mentoring, networking, providing a sense of support or belonging, and encouraging junior professors with their research proposals and writing projects.

Unfortunately, collegiality is not well developed at many academic institutions and is too seldom a part of junior faculty development. In my study (Jarvis, 1991), one of Stanford's energetic junior professors offered this assessment of the situation: "Among most faculty members, warmth is often hidden because of the briefcase mentality. There's never any time to talk. It's like an ad from the *New Yorker*. The ideal setup seems to be a townhouse in Santa Barbara, a BMW to take you to campus to dispense your wisdom and then as quickly to whisk you back home to your word processor. The new faculty are very detached and cynical. It gives me physical discomfort in the gut." Turner and Boice (1987a, pp. 6–7) reported similar findings from a study of new faculty at a large regional university on the West Coast: "Relationships with colleagues were the most salient and pervasive source of dissatisfaction. . . . The inexperienced were indignant and largely convinced that it was a local problem; the experienced were more cynical than angry; the reentry were both confused and disappointed; the lecturers were convinced that it was a result of their second-class status." Clearly, collegiality is a problem for junior faculty members.

Tactics for Developing Junior Faculty Scholarship

In the following sections, I review tactics for developing collegiality and explore more general issues in successful faculty development programs.

Mentoring. Mentoring is one way of improving both collegiality and junior faculty research. Zuckerman (1977) found the social ties between older and younger Nobel laureates to be "ensuring and consequential." She found not only that there was a significant number of familial bonds among Nobel recipients but also that "more than half (forty-eight) of the ninety-two laureates who did their prize-winning research in the United States by 1972 had worked either as students, postdoctorates, or junior collaborators under older Nobel laureates" (1977, pp. 99–100). Ten laureate masters helped to produce thirty American recipients. The English physicists J. J. Thompson and Ernest Rutherford taught between them a total of seventeen recipients. While simple teacher-student relationships may have been a factor with these Nobel laureates, it is clear that more complex mentoring, a socialization into new ways of thinking about their disciplines and themselves, as well as the nomination process, played a significant role in the development of these famous scientists. Zuckerman noted that "the least important aspect of their apprenticeship was the acquiring of substantive knowledge from their master"; far more important were the mentors' modes of thinking, their standards of excellence, and, most important, the self-confidence that the masters instilled in their apprentices (pp. 122–123). Relationships of this kind are just as effective in the humanities: Well over one-half of my informants, especially the publishing scholars, felt that mentors in graduate school or later were important in their own development. Scholars mentioned mentors as important far more frequently than did the teachers and administrators (Jarvis, 1991).

Administrators cannot guarantee that all mentoring attempts will succeed, but they can do much to facilitate mentoring. Top-echelon academic leaders can ask their subordinates what they are doing to encourage collegiality and mentoring: It is useful merely to raise the issue and let all of the institution's leaders know that this is an important subject on which they should be exercising their own fertile imaginations. Senior faculty and development experts can collaborate to set up formal mentoring programs. At the very least, department chairs can remind their best senior professors that collegiality is an important and satisfying aspect of their responsibility as members of a community of scholars. Most will be receptive to the idea, because as adults mature, the majority develop a greater interest in what Erikson (1959, p. 97) called "generativity," the helping and fostering activities necessary to bring along the next generation.

Mentoring has played a key role in a number of junior faculty development programs, including those of the Lilly Endowment, Beloit College, GLCA, and California State University at Long Beach. The organizers of the

Long Beach program, which studied mentoring pairs, emphasized mandatory weekly meetings of the pairs and monthly meetings of all project participants in order to establish a critical mass of collegial interaction (Boice and Turner, 1989). They also discovered that pairings can be successful across disciplines, genders, and age lines. The pairs most often discussed research and publications and next most often discussed teaching.

In the GLCA program, which focuses exclusively on enhancement of research skills, senior faculty members from the constituent colleges of the association were invited to volunteer by submitting applications. Officials tried to match each mentor with an apprentice in the same professional field but employed at a different campus. This difference in locale ensured that the mentors were uninfluenced by circumstances on the apprentices' campuses such as local academic politics. In addition, the outside mentors provided entry into information networks away from the apprentices' campuses ("Professional Development . . . ," 1986). Organizers of the GLCA program reported that success depended on the proximity of the campuses, on the compatibility of the participants, on their willingness to contribute time to the program, and on their desire to deepen a casual professional acquaintance into a mentoring relationship. Apparently, most of the pairings were limited to one or two meetings and follow-up telephone calls.

Mentoring relationships are almost never permanent, however, so considerable discomfort may develop for both members as the apprentice matures and requires more independence (Dalton and Thompson, 1986). This tension can be minimized if the mentor foresees this need for independence and allows the relationship, when appropriate, to become more egalitarian. As John S. Harris, a professor of English at Brigham Young University, told us in an interview, "Mentors should produce protégés, not disciples."

Group Projects. Faculty research expertise can also be facilitated by group projects that encourage collegiality and mentoring. Among the most common group activities under this rubric are departmental, regional, and junior faculty colloquia and research groups. The important features of successful group projects are informal, collegial sharing of ideas; keeping up with the literature; and encouraging future work. Junior professors tend to avoid the more formal colloquia, where they are expected to present finished papers in competition with senior colleagues who eventually will be judging their suitability for tenure.

To foster peer mentoring relationships, leaders can encourage meetings where junior professors talk about the literature, work on projects, or simply socialize. Many of the prominent American professors in my study reported that peer groups were central to their development as scholars. The more successful group projects were commonly limited to junior professors, but younger professionals also found departmental colloquia helpful if a democratic atmosphere prevailed. In neither arrangement were large sums budgeted to keep the groups going, but a little money was available for refreshments, duplication, and publicity (Jarvis, 1991).

One of the simplest and most effective group projects is a lunch-time seminar for new faculty at the University of Oklahoma, in Norman. Begun in fall 1988, the semester-long program involves new faculty members who meet weekly on a voluntary basis for a free lunch followed by a program dedicated to general orientation, teaching, and research. Each session is offered first on Mondays and then again on Thursdays to minimize time conflicts and to keep group size manageable. The organizers report that over 70 percent of eligible new faculty attended regularly (Fink, 1989, this volume).

Research Centers. A number of research universities have established research centers for traditionally underfunded subject areas such as the humanities that lack the disciplinary incentives of the sciences for researchers to work together in teams. These research centers provide offices and reductions in teaching loads for six to ten faculty members during a year's fellowship. The centers frequently reserve a few slots each year for junior professors and usually require monthly or weekly meetings in which the fellows share work-in-progress reports. Junior and senior faculty members who have participated as fellows in such centers usually appreciated the released time, but their highest praise is reserved for the collegiality and the exchange of ideas, which they found immensely helpful and stimulating (Jarvis, 1991).

Travel Money. Travel money is an obvious and important aspect of junior faculty research development because it allows junior professors to make contacts outside of their institutions with other scholars in their research specialties. Paradoxically, there appears to be an inverse correlation between university prestige and travel money available: The better known the university, the less money there seems to be for travel. Few junior faculty members at any of the best-known research institutions regularly receive enough funding to cover the cost of travel and lodging (or meals) at even one national conference each year. Whatever the rationale of such a policy for well-paid senior professors at famous research centers, this stinginess with travel money has a devastating effect on the many junior professors who lack both travel funding and its substitute: personal acquaintances at other universities to whom the young researchers could write or telephone for research ideas and advice. More disturbing is the evidence that second-tier but ambitious universities are following the prestigious institutions' lead by cutting travel funds whenever possible. When selecting a university position, young academics should carefully consider availability of travel funds as a critical aspect of their development.

Time to Research. Time to research is another important advantage for junior professors as well as for senior professors. One-half of the publishing scholars in my survey mentioned early leaves as having been important to their success, and time to research is consistently one of the most frequently recommended aids to junior faculty development. Turner and Boice (1987b) reported that most junior faculty members at a large state university were highly motivated to be productive scholars, but few found the time that they thought necessary for their research: Most hoped to spend 50 percent of their time on scholarship but actually spent less than 15 percent on it, and many finished no papers the first year. To help junior professors increase their publication rates, Turner and Boice advocated helping junior professors use short, regular blocks of time productively. Boice (1984, p. 198) reported success in helping senior "distressed" faculty members improve their writing output by means of a program "with priorities on brief, daily periods of undisrupted writing and on completion and submission of scholarly writing projects."

Most of the prominent publishing scholars in my study were able to use short blocks of time, and they saw that ability as important to their success. Stanford historian Louis Spitz recalled a stuffy instructor at the University of Chicago who admonished his students, "Ladies and Gentlemen! Utilize the interstices." While agreeing that only a pedant would put it that way, Spitz felt that the basic idea is sound: The ability to use short blocks of time is a significant advantage. However, a significant minority of the best scholars insisted that large blocks of time were necessary for their writing. Yale's Edmund Morgan welcomed large blocks but advised that scholars have to keep their "hand in research all the time, or there's too much floundering around when the free semester comes up." He claimed to be able to research faster than he could absorb the information and insisted, "I need time to think about it, sort it through." Perhaps the correct conclusion here is that only a minority need large blocks of time, and all ought to use regularly the shorter blocks of time at their disposal.

Three studies suggest that there is such a thing as too much time for research: Pelz and Andrews first proposed this in 1966, Knorr and colleagues later supplied corroboration (see Creswell, 1979), and, finally, Boice (1987) sharply criticized released time as unproductive. Knorr found that productivity was highest when about one-third of a scientist's time was available for research, the reminder for teaching or administration. Similarly, Turner and Boice (1987b) found that lecturers, despite their heavier teaching load, produced as many papers and articles for publication as did new tenure track faculty.

In summary, I recommend that junior professors be provided reasonable amounts of time for research; however, the use of more than about one-third of their time for research may produce diminishing returns. If scholars can learn to use regularly the available time in their schedules, research time need not necessarily be sought in large blocks.

Financial Support. Nearly one-half of my informants mentioned that financial support for research was currently provided for junior faculties of their institutions (this proportion is probably higher in the sciences). This funding includes summer and academic year support; research, editing, and typing assistance; and local matching of outside grants to provide a little extra money for overhead and the like. A small but vehement number of humanities professors said that they wanted their campus research offices to give them more help with research proposals in their areas. Apparently, these research support personnel are more familiar with funding agencies in the sciences than in the humanities. Several of the humanist informants complained that their local research offices are about as helpful as "sand in the gears."

Facilities and Equipment. Proper facilities and equipment are, of course, essential to most types of research. Scientists are so reliant on elaborate equipment that they have a hard time understanding how humanists have made do for so long with nothing more than a few great books, yellow pads, and wooden pencils. Significant work will doubtless be done yet in the future with nothing more than these basics, but junior faculty members in every field should have ready access to computers—for word processing, if nothing else—and willing assistance from computer experts who also understand the professors' fields, since commercial software packages seldom meet all of the arcane needs of academics. Computers are usually more useful if they can be linked to local and national data bases. A number of other electronic media are becoming increasingly useful for research: videotapes, video disks, and television satellite antennae. Acquisition and retrievable storage of these important nonprint media are seldom coordinated in any rational fashion on any campus, although there is ample reason for them to be easily accessible for both research and pedagogical purposes.

Maintenance. Maintenance of offices, classrooms, and laboratories is not something most young academics would consider in choosing a first place to work, but it is becoming a sore point on some campuses. At one prestigious research university, preventive maintenance seems to have been severely constrained for several years, and even custodial work is now apparently limited to the emptying of wastebaskets only after they overflow. A junior faculty member at that university spent a Memorial Day weekend in the hospital after being bitten by one of the hundreds of spiders in her office; elsewhere on that campus, a mouse in a departmental commons has been in residence so long that faculty members considered nominating it for tenure. Clearly, the maintenance issue is much larger than junior faculty development and involves important, knotty issues of funding priorities, but it is a factor that junior faculty candidates should weigh along with other considerations.

Summary

Programs to further develop junior faculty research skills are clearly needed because first employment positions affect professors' later careers more than do their graduate schools, and the habit of research and writing must be established early if it is ever to be established. Effective programs for junior faculty development are characterized by firm administrative support, good management, good communication, an orientation toward the future, and—most important—collegiality, because research is not usually a lone effort but is largely a product of "evocative environments" in a community of scholars.

Tactics for developing junior faculty research skills include mentoring, group projects, travel money to interact with the larger community of scholars, a reasonable (but not excessive) amount of research time in short blocks, research support programs, and good facilities, equipment, and maintenance.

References

Boice, R. "Coping with Difficult Colleagues." *Department Advisor*, 1973, 2 (4), 5–8.

Boice, R. "Reexamination of Traditional Emphases in Faculty Development." *Research in Higher Education*, 1984, 21 (2), 195–209.

Boice, R. "Is Released Time an Effective Component of Faculty Development Programs?" *Research in Higher Education*, 1987, 26 (3), 311–326.

Boice, R., and Turner, J. L. "The FIPSE-CSULB Mentoring Project for New Faculty." *To Improve the Academy*, 1989, 8, 117–139.

Bowen, H. R., and Schuster, J. H. *American Professors: A National Resource Imperiled.* New York: Oxford University Press, 1986.

"Campus Research." *Wall Street Journal*, Nov. 29, 1985, sec. 2, p. 15.

Creswell, J. W. *Faculty Research Performance: Lessons from the Sciences and the Social Sciences.* ASHE-ERIC Higher Education Reports, no. 4. Washington, D.C.: Association for the Study of Higher Education, 1985.

Dalton, G., and Thompson, P. *Novations: Strategies for Career Management.* Glenview, Ill.: Scott, Foresman, 1986.

Erikson, E. H. "Growth and Crisis of the Healthy Personality." In E. H. Erikson (ed.), *Identity and the Life Cycle.* New York: International Universities Press, 1959.

Fink, L. D. "Oklahoma Professional Development Seminar: An Assessment of Its First Year." Paper presented at the conference of the Professional and Organizational Development Network in Higher Education, Jekyll Island, Georgia, October 5–8, 1989.

Jarvis, D. K. *Junior Faculty Development: A Handbook.* New York: Modern Language Association, 1991.

"Professional Development: Bringing New Faculty on Board." *Academic Leader*, 1986, 2 (8), 1–2.

Siegel, M. E. "Empirical Findings on Faculty Development Programs." In W. C. Nelson and M. E. Siegel (eds.), *Effective Approaches to Faculty Development.* Washington, D.C.: Association of American Colleges, 1980.

Turner, J. L., and Boice, R. "A Longitudinal Study of Faculty Careers." Paper presented at the annual meeting of the Western Psychological Association, Long Beach, California, April 25, 1987a.

Turner, J. L., and Boice, R. "Starting at the Beginning: The Concerns and Needs of New Faculty." *To Improve the Academy*, 1987b, 6, 41–55.

Zuckerman, H. *Scientific Elite: Nobel Laureates in the United States.* New York: Free Press, 1977.

DONALD K. JARVIS *is professor of Russian at Brigham Young University, Provo, Utah, where he previously served as dean of general education and chair of Asian and Slavic Languages. He is the author of* Junior Faculty Development: A Handbook *(New York: Modern Language Association, 1991).*

The Lilly Endowment Teaching Fellows Program has been
successful in helping junior faculty improve their teaching
and become socialized to the professorial role.

Supporting Junior Faculty Through a Teaching Fellows Program

Ann E. Austin

The challenges of teaching effectively loom large for new and junior faculty, many of whom have had little formal preparation for this aspect of their professorial role. For more than a decade and a half, at more than forty major universities, the Lilly Endowment has sponsored a teaching fellows program for faculty in the pretenure years. The program's explicit purpose is to provide a vehicle through which junior faculty members can develop their expertise as teachers as they also establish themselves as researchers and writers. The Lilly Endowment Teaching Fellows Program is especially noteworthy, however, for the way that it addresses not only the teaching-related concerns of junior faculty but also the array of the other challenges confronting them.

A recent evaluation study that I conducted examined the impact of the teaching fellows program on both the faculty members who have participated and the universities involved (Austin, 1990a, 1990b). Considerable evidence indicates that the program has a significant positive effect on the quality of teaching and the career development of faculty fellows. Additionally (although not of primary interest in this chapter), at many of the participating universities, the teaching fellows program had led to the establishment or expansion of other institutional programs to support teaching excellence.

In this chapter, I begin with a description of the components of the Lilly Endowment Teaching Fellows Program. Then, I discuss how and why this program is a particularly effective way to support the professional development of junior faculty. Finally, I identify critical organizational factors that relate to the degree of impact and success achieved by this kind of program.

The Lilly Endowment Teaching Fellows Program

Since 1974, the Lilly Endowment has selected several universities each year to receive one-year grants to develop teaching fellows programs. While the grants are nearly always renewable for up to three years, the endowment strongly urges the universities to contribute in increasing amounts over the three years so that they are prepared to assume full financial support of their programs at the termination of external funding. About one-third of the universities that have received Lilly Endowment support have contributed the programs on their own; additionally, some universities, while not continuing teaching fellows programs, have supported other teaching-related activities that have their roots in the Lilly program.

A teaching fellows program typically involves six to ten tenure-stream junior faculty members who are appointed as fellows for a one-year term. Usually, fellows have been at the institution between one and five years; faculty in their first year are generally not eligible, on the assumption that they are busy with initial acclimation to their new environments. Some participants may have taught a short while elsewhere but are new to the current institution and untenured. (While the endowment focuses its support on untenured faculty, some universities that have maintained teaching fellows programs for a number of years have expanded eligibility to faculty at any rank. Generally, however, the program is designed for junior faculty.)

The process of appointing fellows varies by institution, but usually a selection committee reviews applications and nominations. Members of the committee often include the program director, program advisory board members, university senior administrative leaders, members of committees dealing with teaching issues, and previous fellows. Virtually all of the programs require written applications, and some ask for interviews and project proposals. Each group of fellows includes faculty members from a range of disciplines and fields.

Although all teaching fellows programs are designed to support fellows as they develop as teachers, programs vary in their emphases. Some deal broadly and philosophically with teaching and career issues of interest to junior faculty; others take a very practical approach to the methods and approaches useful in teaching at the postsecondary level. Furthermore, programs differ in their levels of structure. Some programs are quite structured, such as those at Syracuse University and at the University of Rhode Island, with the program directors essentially offering a course on teaching. Others, such as the University of Rochester program, are unstructured in the sense of expecting each new group of fellows to set its own agenda. Which approach is more beneficial and appropriate depends on each institution's goals for the program as well as on the availability and kinds of other resources that contribute to junior faculty development. While each university receiving Lilly support develops its own plan for the program and while programs evolve as they continue over a number of years, several basic elements are included in typical teaching fellows programs.

Regular Group Meetings. Regular interaction among the fellows is a key ingredient in the program. Meetings typically occur once or twice a month, often over lunch or dinner. Through ongoing social and professional interaction, fellows come to know each other well, develop the trust necessary to engage in open conversation about teaching and career concerns, and learn about events and issues in other parts of the university. Topics for group discussion vary depending on the goals and structure of each program. Examples of topics include the characteristics and needs of different groups of students, specific teaching methods and their applicability, theories of student development, and analysis of current or classic books concerning teaching. Some meetings might be devoted to such career issues as stages of an academic career, tenure and promotion processes, and questions regarding research and publishing. Also, campus issues, policies, and politics are often meeting topics.

Variations on the regular meetings provide additional avenues for conversation and foster the development of group rapport. In some programs, each fellow hosts a "home visit," a regular meeting at which the other fellows go to the host's department to learn about the particularities of teaching in that discipline. Some programs also schedule meetings in the residences of the fellows, where casual interaction can easily occur. In some programs, fellows supplement their regular meetings with periodic lunch discussions of short articles concerning teaching or faculty issues. A late spring or summer orientation meeting attended by both new fellows and the past year's fellows is often used as a link between different cohorts of fellows. Picnics, potlucks, and other social occasions, as well as special opportunities to meet distinguished guests and speakers at the university, can be included in the year's program also.

Individual Projects. During the period when the Lilly Endowment is providing funding, fellows individually carry out teaching-related projects. Although some universities have dropped this component of the program over time, many program directors and fellows cite it as a useful way to support faculty members as they explore their individual interests and to enrich the learning of the whole group through the presentation of each fellow's project. Typical projects may involve designing a new course or redesigning a previously taught course, developing instructional materials (such as computer programs, simulations, or games), or studying an issue related to teaching (such as ways to be more responsive to a pluralistic student body or the usefulness of particular developmental theories in designing teaching approaches). While a number of past fellows have published textbooks or articles that originated in their projects, publication is not the required or expected goal.

Program directors have assumed a variety of roles in regard to fellows' projects. Some leave the fellows on their own to work on the projects, while others take a strong advisory role, perhaps arranging individual meetings every two months to discuss progress on the projects. This contact encourages fellows to take the project component seriously and ensures that fellows are aware of available resources and contacts. Opportunities to share findings or results also increase the likelihood that fellows allocate necessary time for developing and finishing their projects. Some programs build time for progress reports into their regular meetings, others schedule a meeting devoted to final reports, and still others arrange times to invite the whole university community to hear about the fellows' work.

Release Time. When the endowment is supplying funding, fellows must have some release time from their teaching responsibilities. However, when universities assume full program funding, release time sometimes is omitted as a way to save costs. If at all possible, release time from one course during the year or one course each semester is very desirable for several reasons. First, the provision of release time conveys the message that fellows are expected to participate actively in the program and to take seriously their projects, readings, and meetings. Second, release time enables junior faculty members to see the fellowship as a significant and positive opportunity rather than as an additional burden on top of an already crowded schedule. Given the long work hours and heavy press to research that junior faculty experience, the provision of release time can be a critical ingredient in a faculty member's consideration of participating in the program. Third, the provision of a stipend to "buy out" some of the fellows' time is a useful way to legitimate the program in the eyes of department chairs. This is particularly important when a teaching fellows program is new to the campus.

Fellows have reported that actual allocation of release time to fellowship activities, projects, and reading can be difficult to achieve. Multiple demands interfere with good intentions. Some program directors suggest that fellows post a calendar marked with times for fellowship meetings and work on projects to remind themselves and their colleagues that involvement as a fellow represents a significant commitment. Program directors also find that benefits other than release time may be helpful to some fellows. For example, faculty in the sciences often already teach a reduced load but might be able to free up time for the activities of the program if funding for graduate assistant support in their laboratories were provided.

Senior Faculty Mentors. Although some universities with teaching fellows programs have omitted a mentor component, the involvement of senior faculty who serve as mentors to their junior colleagues is often a key part of the programs. Typically, senior faculty selected as mentors are respected as outstanding teachers-scholars. Where mentoring is a component, the patterns vary considerably. Some programs require that the mentor and the fellow with whom he or she works hold appointments in different departments. The intention is to protect the fellows from concern that questions posed or issues raised could be prejudicial to their tenure review. In contrast, other program directors urge fellows to select mentors from their own departments, since the mentor and mentee then share a disciplinary perspective, regular interaction can be arranged more easily, and the senior colleague can help protect the fellow from overly extensive departmental assignments during the fellowship year. A third pattern is one in which fellows are free to select any senior professor as mentor, regardless of departmental affiliation. The teaching fellows program that was in place several years ago at Jackson State University in Mississippi exemplifies a fourth model. A group of fifteen senior faculty members, each respected for his or her teaching expertise, was chosen to comprise a program advisory board. Then, each year's fellows chose mentors from this group. Retired faculty, either from the fellow's department or from another field, are another option. They may have more time available to work with junior faculty members and to participate in the program.

Fellows considering whom to ask to serve as mentor may choose to meet with colleagues and department chairs to discuss the contributions that particular senior faculty might make and with past fellows to hear about their experiences with their mentors. Interviews initiated by fellows with possible mentors are encouraged in some programs. In the choice of mentors, fellows should consider their own goals for the relationship, any departmental or institutional politics that could affect the mentor relationship, and the compatibility of their own schedules with those of potential senior mentors.

The mentor role tends to vary by individual mentor-mentee pair and by institutional program. Some pairs arrange regular meetings to discuss teaching-related issues and to visit each other's classes. There are some instances where a mentor and fellow have engaged in joint research projects. Other pairs find that they never really "mesh," and the relationship remains perfunctory and infrequent. The involvement of mentors in fellows' group activities also varies across programs. At some universities, mentors are invited and urged to attend group meetings and retreats as frequently as possible; at others, mentors are asked to participate in group gatherings only occasionally. Even if mentors do not participate regularly in group meetings, they are better prepared for their role if they are included in the meeting or retreat that starts the year. Furthermore, their attendance at an early meeting is an occasion for the fellows to meet all the mentors and to begin to develop an expanded set of senior faculty colleagues. In some programs, mentors also meet separately with the program directors for orientation to their roles and responsibilities.

While a variety of mentor arrangements have been successful in teaching fellows programs, one factor associated with success is evident: flexibility in approach. In flexible programs, fellows choose mentors on the basis of mutual interests and goals, regardless of the potential mentor's departmental affiliation. While the program directors suggest ways in which fellows and mentors might choose to interact and activities that they might wish to share, the specific dimensions of the relationships are left to each mentor-fellow pair. If a mentor turns out to be less helpful than expected, program directors who take a flexible approach recommend that the fellow simply add a second, more compatible mentor while still keeping the first.

Retreats and Conferences. When the Lilly Endowment is funding a university's teaching fellows program, its fellows participate in a fall and a spring weekend retreat arranged by the endowment. These conferences include sessions on a variety of teaching-related topics, often led by widely respected scholars or teaching experts. Additionally, since the endowment sponsors programs at several universities each year, the Lilly retreats enable fellows from the various campuses to meet and interact with each other.

Given the value of these retreats, a number of programs that have continued without external funding still incorporate retreats into their yearly plans. A one- or two-day retreat, during which fellows meet each other, learn about the program's goals and possible activities, and identify personal plans, often serves as the initial program event. A second day-long or weekend retreat is often scheduled for midyear or in spring. Miami University of Ohio, for example, invites outgoing fellows (called "teaching scholars") and newly appointed scholars to a one-day retreat at a lovely inn in late spring. The outgoing fellows report on their projects and discuss their experiences with the new participants, and the new scholars brainstorm about possible plans and projects. In October, the new group of scholars takes a weekend trip to visit a different college or university, during which they acquaint themselves with a variety of teaching methods and lay out their individual project proposals. At the University of Massachusetts, in Amherst, the program begins with a retreat at an inn in the Berkshire Mountains, during which fellows and mentors meet and plan for the year together. Fellows at the University of Georgia, in Athens, end the year with a trip to an ocean resort where they relax, socialize, discuss issues pertaining to teaching, and report on their year-long projects.

The benefits of these retreats are well worth the time and costs involved. Directors report that new groups of fellows often "jell" as they interact casually while driving to a retreat center, share in meal preparation or other chores, enjoy a pleasant environment, and relax. An off-campus meeting place also removes participants from other important responsibilities that typically vie for their time and can diminish their full attention. Additionally, the experience of spending time at a pleasant site and enjoying good food tells fellows that the university values and is willing to invest in them. Such messages that they are "special" are rare for junior faculty.

Program Variations. Each university puts its own imprint on a teaching fellows program, often adding a unique component or fresh slant to the typical ingredients. Fellows in some programs observe in each others' classes or view videotapes of each other's teaching and engage in group critique and suggestions. Some directors order each fellow a year's subscription to *Change,* a publication sponsored by the American Association for Higher Education, while others provide a reading list at the start of the year that serves as a basis for ongoing group discussion. A few programs allocate funds to enable their fellows as a group to attend the meeting of the American Association for Higher Education, held annually in early spring. At some universities, the teaching fellows programs sponsor conferences on teaching issues to which past fellows, interested colleagues and department chairs, and senior institutional leaders are invited. Such conferences can serve several purposes. Fellows can share some of what they have been learning through presentations or conversations with others attending; the teaching fellows program increases its visibility; junior faculty who have not yet been fellows become acquainted with the program; and the interaction and bonding between past and current fellows strengthens the network of faculty across campus who share a serious interest in teaching.

Costs. Program costs vary depending on whether all the program elements described above are included (for example, whether mentors are involved and receive honoraria, whether meetings regularly occur over a meal, or whether the fellows go to an off-campus retreat site), the numbers of fellows and mentors, and the quality of meals and meeting locations selected. Generally, for a group of seven to ten fellows, a university should plan on an allocation of $30,000 to $50,000 per year. Much of this expenditure typically goes to release time. If release time is limited to one course per fellow or is not provided, costs diminish accordingly. A portion of a program's budget also often goes to underwrite the program director's salary. Criteria for selecting program directors vary across campuses; directors of instructional development or faculty development centers, provosts or other senior institutional leaders, and faculty members interested in faculty development have been program directors. The budget allocated to the program director's salary depends on such factors as whether time is donated and what portion of time is to be used for the program.

Why Is the Teaching Fellows Program Effective?

While it is always difficult to determine the impact of any single experience on a faculty member's career, thorough evaluation of the impact of the Lilly Endowment Teaching Fellows Program at the thirty universities involved between 1974 and 1988 indicated that it was typically a significant and positive experience for the junior faculty participants (Austin, 1990a, 1990b). Approximately 90 percent of the fellows studied reported that the program had a positive long-term impact on their teaching and careers. What makes this program especially effective and successful? The ways in which the program affects fellows provide a clue. Evidence is strong that the program affects junior faculty in four areas in particular: teaching skills and attitudes, collegial contacts, university citizenship, and professional confidence. The literature on the challenges confronting new and junior faculty, which has been reviewed and discussed in detail in earlier chapters of this volume, shows that the concerns and needs of junior faculty are closely matched to these four areas of positive impact.

Teaching Skills and Attitudes. According to the research on new and junior faculty, novices in the professoriate experience great stress from their teaching responsibilities, feel uncertain about how to improve their teaching, and typically have received little guidance in graduate school or from colleagues about creative and effective approaches to teaching (Boice, 1991; Fink, 1984). The Lilly Endowment Teaching Fellows Program directly responds to the need of junior faculty members to learn more about teaching. Fellows, as well as deans, department chairs, and program directors, have reported that the fellowship experience affects both how participants think about teaching as well as how they do their teaching.

Fellows often develop a deeper interest in and commitment to being a good teacher and, through their exposure to theories of teaching and learning, consciously formulate personal philosophies about teaching. For many fellows, the core of their emerging teaching philosophies is a humanism that emphasizes appreciation of student differences, interest in listening to students, and a greater commitment to fostering the process of students' intellectual growth than to dispensing knowledge. Past fellows have reported that they became more attentive to students' learning needs; more sensitive to such barriers as learning disabilities, anxiety, and challenges associated with English as a second language; and more careful about helping students link theoretical concepts and practical problems. This heightened sensitivity to students' diverse needs and challenges, coupled with exploration of teaching and learning theory, often causes fellows to cultivate new approaches to their teaching. Through group meetings and individual projects, fellows learn about creative teaching methods—the use of computers, games, simulations, and cooperative learning, for example—and often develop new instructional materials.

Certainly, participants vary in how they describe the extent of change in their approach to teaching. Some experience dramatic transformations, as expressed by one fellow: "The result was a total transformation of my teaching, and I feel very good about the changes. The most positive thing that I think came from the project is that students now comment on how much they learned rather than how much they *liked* the course" (Austin, 1991b, p. 25). For other fellows, the effects on their teaching are more subtle. But with high frequency, fellows report that the teaching fellowship experience significantly affected how they view the purposes of teaching, their personal commitment to teaching excellence, and the breadth and command of skills and methods used in their teaching.

Collegial Contacts. Conversations with new and junior faculty as well as the systematic research studies on the experiences of these members of the professoriate invariably highlight their sense of isolation and desire to experience more extensive and supportive collegial interaction with other faculty (Boice, 1991; Fink, 1984; Whitt, 1991). The Lilly Endowment Teaching Fellows Program directly addresses this serious concern by offering a structure through which junior faculty fellows meet and develop ongoing collegial relationships with each other and with senior members of the faculty. Since each group of fellows is composed of faculty from different departments, participants learn about issues in other parts of the university and career challenges and teaching practices that vary across disciplines. Even more important for many of the fellows is the opportunity to develop continuing relationships that often blossom into friendships with faculty outside of their own respective fields. Due to myriad responsibilities and the solitary nature of most research and teaching preparation, many faculty members (particularly those in the early years) have little time for extended conversations, even with their colleagues down the hall. It is not surprising, then, that junior faculty typically find that opportunities to cultivate professional relationships with others in different fields are few. The teaching fellows program provides an avenue for these contacts and then fuels their growth. Many fellows report that just discussing their questions and concerns with others in similar circumstances alleviates some of the sense of isolation (Austin, 1991b).

When mentor relationships succeed, they also add significantly to a feeling of colleagueship for the fellows. Senior mentors can provide the kind of feedback and suggestions that many junior faculty need. If a program also includes conferences, seminars, or other events that involve fellows with other members of the university community, it further contributes to collegial support.

University Citizenship. In addition to wanting supportive colleagueship, junior faculty need to know what their institutions expect regarding their work and what resources are available to help them do their work. The Lilly Endowment Teaching Fellows Program also assists participants with this concern. Interactions between fellows and mentors from other departments, coupled with sessions with university leaders, give participants an institutional perspective. Meetings with provosts and deans, for example, often deal explicitly with tenure requirements and recommendations for preparation of promotion dossiers. Program directors also usually arrange opportunities for fellows to learn about institutional resources available to them, such as instructional and curricular resources, personal and professional support services, and funding resources and grant support. Fellows become not only more knowledgeable about the university and its resources but also more visible to senior administrative leaders and faculty, which can lead to appointments on significant institutional committees.

As one past fellow explained, "The program made me knowledgeable about my home institution and introduced me to people within that institution whom I value as friends and colleagues and who make me feel more integrated with the university" (Austin, 1991b, p. 32). Junior faculty who are part of a teaching fellows program become active university citizens—both in terms of their knowledge and their roles—more quickly than do their colleagues who are not participants in the program.

Professional Confidence. Stress from concern about their ability to meet a wide array of personal and professional demands typically pervades the lives of junior faculty (Carnegie Foundation for the Advancement of Teaching, 1989; Finkelstein, 1984; Sorcinelli, 1988; Olsen and Sorcinelli, this volume; Whitt, 1991). It is significant, then, that, for many fellows, participation in the program has led to greater self-confidence, self-esteem, and morale. Some find in the program a way to make a smooth transition from graduate student to faculty member, from uncertainty to confidence. Others find that the program bolsters their confidence that they have the abilities to balance teaching and research and handle both career and family.

Other Impacts. From my extensive evaluation study, the four areas discussed above emerge as the primary ways in which the Lilly Endowment Teaching Fellows Program affects participants. Faculty who have passed through this program praise its benefits because it has helped them to deal with the issues that they found most difficult. While specifically focused on helping junior faculty develop as teachers, the program also meets their other concerns.

Although the evidence is strong that the program has significant positive effects on participants, a small number of past fellows have noted that involvement in a teaching fellows program can divert time from the research work needed to achieve tenure. Most fellows, however, do not believe that their participation hindered their progress toward tenure. Also, for some, heightened commitment to teaching excellence and expanded knowledge about teaching and learning have brought frustration. Fellows come to recognize that good teaching takes time, and some report discomfort with the compromises that sometimes must be made in the face of numerous responsibilities (Austin, 1991b). Perhaps the lesson is that even an excellent faculty development program, designed to assist junior faculty in handling their greatest concerns, cannot alleviate all tensions and stresses inherent to the professorial role.

Organizational Factors Associated with Successful Programs

Successful teaching fellows programs help junior faculty to be more competent in their teaching, more responsive to student needs, more professionally self-confident, and more connected to colleagues. Additionally, in concert with other university programs and emphases, successful programs reinforce institutional commitment to teaching excellence. While this chapter describes typical aspects of a teaching fellows program, each university must adapt the general model to its own institutional circumstances and culture as well as to the particular needs and interests of each year's fellows. In some universities, for example, a highly structured program is well received, while in others a more flexible approach better responds to faculty interests. Also, themes or emphases in program planning can parallel or build on institutionwide initiatives. For example, a university making an institutional commitment to better meeting the needs of a diverse population might encourage fellows to develop projects on social pluralism and might organize meetings around this theme.

In addition to the importance of tailoring program plans to a university's culture and goals, several other factors also are associated with successful teaching fellows programs. These include supportive institutional leaders, a committed director, wide institutional support, and the cultivation of community among groups of fellows.

Supportive Institutional Leaders. Senior administrative leaders, including presidents, provosts, and deans, play a central role in conveying the message that the university both is concerned about its junior faculty and supports programs that assist these faculty. In fact, my evaluation study of teaching fellows programs indicates that senior leaders who are committed advocates and are able to influence budget allocations are critically important to the survival of these programs. One example is provided by the University of Massachusetts, where, even in the midst of serious financial constraints, the teaching fellows program has continued without external funding and, additionally, a center for teaching has been established. This success owes much to the considerable involvement of the associate vice chancellor for academic affairs in the program, especially during its earliest years, and his strong public advocacy of the importance of teaching at the institution and the contribution made by the teaching fellows program.

Directors of teaching fellows programs can cultivate the continuing support of senior leaders by keeping them well informed about the fellows and their activities and accomplishments, program activities and projects, evidence of the impact of the programs on the participants and the institutions, and any other faculty development activities different from but with roots in the teaching fellows programs. Directors also find it beneficial to invite institutional leaders to each year's initial meeting and periodically to extend invitations to special occasions during which they can meet and interact with the fellows.

A Committed, Conscientious Director. Much of the overall success of a teaching fellows program and the individual successes of the participants rest on the dedication, interest, and hard work of the program director. An effective director is highly committed to the program and its purposes, understands the challenges that confront junior faculty, and is able to secure budget allocations for the program each year. Additionally, the individual appointed as director is more effective if he or she is widely respected as a teacher-scholar, has rapport with senior-level administrators, and exhibits warmth, tact, accessibility, and trustworthiness.

Typically, directors are senior administrators, leaders of faculty development or teaching centers, or interested faculty members. Directors in each of these roles have advantages and disadvantages. For example, a senior-level administrator may have considerable input into budget allocation, but significant limits on available time to meet with fellows collectively or individually. A director of a teaching center is likely to bring to the job much expertise about teaching and junior faculty and knowledge about useful resource people but may not be as widely known across campus as a senior administrator. Similarly, a faculty member may not be widely known but may bring essential enthusiasm and vision to the program. Wide recognition of the director can help a newly developing program achieve legitimacy and visibility. Regardless of the director's institutional position, however, he or she must exhibit the qualities outlined above.

Wide Institutional Support. In order for a faculty development strategy such as a teaching fellows program to achieve viability and durability, a base of support across the institution must be developed. Faculty, administrators, and students must be aware of the program and see it as prestigious and important. To increase awareness, the program director can visit department chairpersons to discuss the program, send activity updates to administrative leaders and department heads, arrange for newspaper coverage of the incoming fellows, their projects, and special events, and nominate fellows and past fellows for teaching awards and committees that deal with teaching-related issues. The practices of involving different senior faculty as mentors each year and appointing an advisory board of influential and interested members of the university can also help to spread word about the program.

Several universities have developed special events that both inform the university communities about the teaching fellows programs and serve as forums for exchange of teaching ideas. For example, some programs sponsor teaching conferences open to all faculty, at which fellows lead sessions based on what they have been learning. The University of Massachusetts holds a "Celebration of Teaching" dinner each year to which fellows, mentors, other faculty who have received teaching awards, university and state leaders, and selected students are invited. The highlight of this distinguished event is the period during which each fellow discusses what he or she has gained from the fellowship experience.

The visibility of programs is not the only important factor. Successful programs also constantly carry the message that they are prestigious. They emphasize excellence and in no way appear remedial. Few faculty members want to identify themselves as in need of remedial assistance; rather, selection as a fellow should be seen as an honor, the result of a competitive process. Also, the involvement of highly respected senior teachers-scholars as mentors enhances the visibility, respect, and prestige associated with the programs.

Another way to enhance the respect accorded to a program is to ensure that all details are "first class." Informative and attractive brochures, a program logo and color scheme, and inviting meals served at program events are seemingly small but nevertheless significant messages about the university's interest in the program specifically and the welfare of junior faculty more broadly.

Creation and Cultivation of Community. When fellows from different years of a program develop networks, collegial connections, or friendships, the benefits of the teaching fellows program, especially its success in diminishing isolation and cultivating colleagueship, are extended. Additionally, a community of past participants can support the continuing work of the program and keep alive within the university some of the issues discussed during the fellowship experience. The director can encourage the creation of networks by inviting past fellows to participate in current program activities and events. For example, a number of programs invite new fellows to meet with outgoing fellows in late spring. Social events such as picnics, dinners, and end-of-year roasts to spoof teaching problems and fellows are other strategies for cultivating connections among fellows across the years of the programs.

Summary

Teaching fellows programs have proved to be a very effective strategy for helping junior faculty both to develop as teachers and to handle some of the other challenges confronting them. Although the support that the Lilly Endowment has provided at a number of universities is very helpful in initiating these programs and is much appreciated, universities can establish successful teaching fellows programs without external assistance.

We might question whether these programs are limited in impact, given the relatively small number of participants at a campus each year. If a teaching fellows program continues over a period of years, however, a number of faculty across departments will have participated, thus creating a network across campus of individuals with a developed expertise in teaching. Also, the program can be viewed as one option within a wide array of faculty development strategies from which junior faculty can choose. Those interested in the teaching fellows program would be individuals willing to make a significant time commitment to development as teachers. Finally, a university might establish several groups of teaching fellows, thus retaining the benefits of small group interaction while also offering the experience to a larger number of junior faculty.

References

Austin, A. E. "Supporting the Professor as Teacher: An Evaluation Study of the Lilly Teaching Fellows Program." Paper presented at the 15th annual meeting of the Association for the Study of Higher Education, Portland, Oregon, November, 1990a.

Austin, A. E. *To Leave an Indelible Mark: Encouraging Good Teaching in Research Universities Through Faculty Development. A Study of the Lilly Endowment's Teaching Fellows Program, 1974–1988.* Nashville, Tenn.: Peabody College, Vanderbilt University, 1990b.

Boice, R. "New Faculty as Teachers." *Journal of Higher Education,* 1991, 62 (2), 150–173.

Carnegie Foundation for the Advancement of Teaching. *The Condition of the Professoriate: Attitudes and Trends, 1989.* Princeton, N.J.: Carnegie Foundation for the Advancement of Teaching, 1989.

Fink, L. D. (ed.). *The First Year of College Teaching.* New Directions for Teaching and Learning, no. 17. San Francisco: Jossey-Bass, 1984.

Finkelstein, M. J. *The American Academic Profession.* Columbus: Ohio State University Press, 1984.

Sorcinelli, M. D. "Satisfactions and Concerns of New University Teachers." *To Improve the Academy,* 1988, 7, 121–131.

Whitt, E. J. " 'Hit the Ground Running': Experiences of New Faculty in a School of Education." *Review of Higher Education,* 1991, 14 (2), 177–197.

ANN E. AUSTIN *is associate professor in the Department of Educational Administration at Michigan State University, East Lansing.*

Department chairpersons can facilitate the success of junior faculty members through the use of a variety of strategies.

The Role of the Chairperson in Support of Junior Faculty

Daniel W. Wheeler

Department chairs at some seventy institutions across the United States identified one of their top priorities as helping new and junior faculty achieve success (Creswell and others, 1990). One of the chairs, from a research university, emphasized the importance of investing time, energy, and resources in new and junior faculty: "It's the responsibility of the department chair to help new faculty succeed. When we recruit an individual, we are convinced that this person has the skills that will really benefit our program. Our responsibility, once we hire, is to provide him or her with the resources and support to be successful."

This chapter draws on my consultations with many chairs about issues confronting junior faculty and strategies for success. The premise of the chapter is that chairs can help junior faculty acclimate to the institution and can provide guidance to enhance their likelihood of success. The enormous investment of time and resources involved in hiring new faculty members makes the provision of support for these junior colleagues an important aspect of the department chair's role. This chapter posits that a chairperson can facilitate the success of junior faculty members by identifying their needs, examining the potential roles in which he or she can be helpful, and taking specific actions and using a number of concrete activities to support junior faculty.

If a chairperson addresses these three facets of working with junior

This chapter is based on the National Chairperson Study, conducted from 1986 to 1988 and supported by the Lilly Foundation and the Teachers Insurance and Annuity Association–College Retirement Equities Fund.

faculty members, the levels of their achievement and advancement can be greatly enhanced. Without systematic attention, the "sink-or-swim" model will prevail, a result that can be costly both to individual faculty members and to the institution.

Junior Faculty Needs

Research on junior faculty (Boice, 1991; Fink, 1984; Sorcinelli, 1989) and the role of chairpersons in faculty development (Creswell and others, 1990) suggests that all faculty members need to develop the following expertise and abilities:

Understanding Institutional Roles and Expectations. The institutional context greatly affects the roles and expectations of faculty. Considerable clarification may occur during the hiring process, but many junior faculty members contend that often the expectations of their departments and the institution are unclear, or worse, in conflict. Whatever the expectations for junior faculty, they should be clear and mutually accepted.

Learning How the Institution Operates in Getting Things Done. New faculty members must find out how to get things done on campus. The best of their ideas may not come to fruition because they lack an understanding of policies and procedures, written and unwritten, and are unaware of the most appropriate channels for achieving results.

Finding Resources. Many kinds of resources are necessary for faculty members to progress professionally. Library, laboratory, and various support services are just a few. Departmental, disciplinary, and institutional expectations determine the press for additional financial resources. For example, to begin a research program in the sciences, junior faculty may be faced with the need for $100,000 to $300,000 to develop a laboratory and obtain the necessary equipment. This can be a daunting task.

Developing Collegiality. New junior faculty consistently indicate that positive working relationships with fellow faculty members are an important aspect of their careers. Yet, work by Boice (1991) and Sorcinelli (1989) suggests that the desire often goes unfulfilled and these connections are not achieved. Boice adds that lack of collegiality may be an even greater problem for minorities and women. This lack of explicit support from established colleagues may be due either to a philosophy that new faculty need to stand on their own or to the fear of established faculty that suggestions for collaboration will be treated as intrusions unless they are requested by the new faculty members.

Obtaining Feedback on Professional Progress. Academics are fiercely independent and often skeptical about evaluation, but they do want feedback about their progress. New faculty are especially concerned about early evaluation of their teaching and progress in research. Heightened anxiety results from lack of feedback or the expectation that "no news is good news." Insufficient feedback can create difficulty down the road when colleagues and administrators need to make personnel decisions.

Improving Skills and Performance in Professional Roles. Ongoing professional development is critical to junior faculty. Strategies for growth in teaching and instructional skills are addressed at some professional society meetings. However, researchers (Creswell and others, 1990; Fink, 1984) have found that many junior faculty need additional interventions to become effective teachers.

Finding a Balance in Work-Life Expectations. Junior faculty express frustration that their lives are consumed by their careers (Sorcinelli and Near, 1989). Particularly with the tight timelines for tenure decisions, faculty may experience alienation from "significant others" and burnout. The necessity of carving out time for family, relationships, leisure, and community activities needs to be recognized and addressed during these initial years.

Potential Chairperson Roles

Given the range of junior faculty needs, chairs can take on several important roles to help facilitate progress in the early years of colleagues' careers. Each of these roles should be considered, although no single chair is likely to be able or willing to attend to all of them. The following are major roles that chairpersons can assume.

Chair as Resource Link. Tucker (1984) characterized the importance of this role in his work on department chairs. Whether referred to as *broker* or *matchmaker*, the role of making a connection between junior faculty resources and resource people is crucial both within the university and in the community at large. Chairs can address some faculty needs for information and understanding of the context of the institution and community through orientation sessions. But because orientation is an ongoing process that requires constant facilitation rather than a one-time activity, chairs should think through some of the following questions.

What orientation resources and information beyond the department are available to faculty? Is there a campuswide new faculty orientation in which faculty are given information about available programs and policies as well as an opportunity to meet other new faculty with similar concerns? Does the chair encourage attendance at these activities for new faculty? Timeliness for these activities is critical; many opportunities will not have the same value several years into the career.

What will be the chair's role in a departmental orientation? Some chairs design a whole sequence of departmental sessions to address issues that they know junior faculty will have to face. Such formal orientations often include information about academic performance standards, policies and practices for working with graduate students, possible funds for research and issues related to the pursuit of grants, effective teaching techniques, important record keeping, faculty service responsibilities, duties of department heads, tenure and promotion, and library resources. Chairs may include information on issues not addressed by other orientations such as student services, benefits and personnel, purchasing, and the physical plant.

Some chairs develop and present an orientation on their own, while others draw on campus resource people. One advantage of introducing junior faculty to resource people is that the newcomers have an opportunity to meet individuals face to face before actually calling them to request services.

Other chairs, especially those from smaller departments or institutions, believe that they can provide an orientation by "meeting around the coffee pot" or dropping in to visit new junior faculty members in their offices. Informal get-togethers can be powerful tools in building relationships but are often overlooked because of the press of time or the lack of initiative by either the chair or the junior faculty members.

A combination of both formal and informal activities, including mentoring, seems to be the best orientation strategy. Effective chairs ensure that departmental orientation efforts have high priority and are maintained throughout the early years of faculty members' careers.

Chair as Mentor. Many chairpersons see themselves as mentors for junior faculty. Certainly, many have accepted the role of department chair because of their interest in working with others. In some ways, chairs make for good mentors because of their knowledge of the ways in which the institution operates and of what it takes to be successful. Also their commitment to new faculty members often develops early in the hiring process.

On the other hand, there are complications in mentoring relationships between the chair and junior faculty. New faculty may feel intimidated by and insecure with the chair, who not only hired them but also is probably responsible for their evaluation. For chairs to be successful as mentors, they must be clear with mentees about their responsibilities to provide both support and evaluation. Straightforward discussion is necessary to head off potential conflicts between the roles of mentor and chair.

Chair as Facilitator of Mentor Relationships. A number of chairpersons have initiated procedures or structures to encourage senior colleagues within their departments to take on mentoring roles. Some departments assign faculty members to serve as mentors, and others provide various opportunities for new faculty to select a mentor or sometimes multiple mentors. In research on the socialization of new junior faculty, Egly (1991) found that junior faculty often have more than one mentor, each of whom is associated with a particular function: teaching, research, service, or career development.

Chair as Institutional Authority or Representative. The department chair is often the first institutional representative who defines and negotiates what the institution expects of faculty. The chair thus plays a crucial role in the development of verbal and written correspondence that pertain to, but are not limited to, job descriptions, written contracts, and job offers.

Clarification of expectations is always important, but it becomes critical in institutions that are in the midst of change. An instructive example is the comprehensive university, which historically has had a primarily undergraduate teaching focus but more recently has emphasized the development of its graduate programs. For both new and senior faculty, stress abounds. Both groups face heavy teaching loads, new demands for research activity, and shortages in institutionally available research resources. Senior faculty often feel conflict because they were hired primarily as teachers but now face new expectations. Some of these long-term faculty complain that "the rules of the game have changed." They feel alienated from the administration, the new institutional emphasis on research, and, often, the institution as a whole.

At the same time, new faculty members in this situation need counsel on "navigating the muddy waters," especially when they hear conflicting views from their peers and the administration. Chairs can help to set priorities, provide reinforcement to the junior faculty member who says no to a request that does not fit priorities, and serve as an advocate for junior faculty members with senior colleagues and higher administrators who will eventually make decisions on tenure and promotion. In short, for junior faculty, protection from distractions and minutia is helpful, and reminders and clarifications of what is expected in order to be successful and remain at the institution are necessary. As one chair exclaimed, "Without some protection, new faculty can become cannon fodder." Even in the most straightforward situations with congruent expectations, guidance of junior faculty by the department chair can prevent missteps and distractions from priorities.

Chair as Evaluator. Chairpersons play a major role in helping junior faculty assess their own progress. New faculty members typically understand what progress means in their respective disciplines or content areas, but the tasks of identifying the institutional benchmarks for progress in teaching, establishing research programs, and meeting other departmental and institutional expectations may be difficult.

Chairs need proficiency in giving specific feedback, coaching on a short-term basis, and conducting annual evaluation conferences. For instance, new faculty often initially spend an inordinate amount of time preparing for their classes. Chairs can demonstrate ways to shorten preparation time and ensure that effective teaching is achieved in an efficient manner.

In the research conducted by Creswell and others (1990), a priority constantly stated by chairs was to be honest and direct in evaluation and other interactions with junior faculty. Their view was that inflated assessments and avoidance of difficult issues caused complications later when hard decisions (such as tenure and promotion) must be made. Without honest feedback, junior faculty members become confused and unclear about their status and progress. As a result, unfavorable decisions may be blamed on politics or personality conflicts rather than on substantiated records of unmet performance expectations.

Certainly, some faculty will not succeed or may be mismatched in terms of personal and institutional goals. For example, an individual who is a successful teacher but a less than enthusiastic researcher may be better placed at an institution that focuses primarily on teaching. The chair can help the junior faculty member make a realistic assessment of his or her strengths and weaknesses and, if necessary, facilitate redirection to a more appropriate institution.

Chair as Faculty Developer. Chairpersons can help directly, provide referral to other professors in the department, or link new faculty to instructional or faculty development centers. To give appropriate referrals, a department chair must be aware of the abilities of all faculty in the department as well as familiar with campus resource people who can provide help. The chair's attitude about a faculty member seeking help is critical. If the chair conveys the attitude that a referral is remedial, rather than a stage through which most new faculty progress, newcomers will be hesitant to reach out for help. What is to be avoided at all costs is a new faculty member who waits until the situation is so desperate and demoralizing that radical interventions are necessary.

If the chairperson chooses to be a direct developer, then refined consulting skills are required. Lucas (1989, 1990) and Creswell and others (1990) provide many strategies and suggestions to chairs for developing effective teaching among junior faculty. One strategy is to visit the classroom, and perhaps videotape the activities, with subsequent feedback to the faculty member regarding particular aspects of teaching and learning. Detailed teaching consultation strategies are provided in Lewis and Povlacs (1988), and numerous suggestions about course structure and classroom operations are offered by McKeachie (1986).

In a more generic vein, Creswell and others (1990) suggest a series of steps through which chairs can stay in tune with faculty on any situation or problem and help them address any needed changes. The steps are to (1) detect the signs of faculty needs, (2) explore the options individually with the person, (3) collaboratively develop a plan for action, and (4) enact the plan and monitor its results.

Beyond these four steps, the practice of staying in touch with new faculty requires a developmental perspective and an awareness that while faculty have many common concerns, they also have unique needs that can be determined through careful observations and in-depth conversations.

Baldwin (1990), Schuster, Wheeler, and Associates (1990), Bowen and Schuster (1986), Menges (1985), Baldwin and Blackburn (1981), and Mathis (1979) provide a solid grounding in the assessment of concerns and stages associated with the development of faculty.

Skill in listening to faculty also was found by Creswell and others (1990) to be crucial for the chairperson as developer. Chairs in their study suggested questions such as "What do you want to do?" and "How can I help you do it?" to increase the exchange of information and to identify ways to be of assistance. Whatever the questions or strategies employed, direct interactions in a supportive atmosphere help to prevent misconceptions or improper assumptions. They also help build trust and good faith, which can provide a basis to overcome what at times seem insurmountable difficulties to newcomers. These are high expectations for chairs, but the times demand new levels of skill and commitment to attract and retain quality junior faculty.

Chair as Model of Balance. Academic careers have the potential to consume new faculty members in the absence of guidance from institutional authorities or admired colleagues. Efforts are needed to prevent faculty burnout and alienation of family members. Chairs can encourage junior faculty to make time for family and themselves, to build it into their schedules. To be sure, many chairs also have difficulty in achieving balance between their academic and personal lives, but those who are able to model this strategy not only benefit personally but are able as well to make the expectation believable to their junior colleagues.

Support Mechanisms and Actions

As outlined above, the chair should try on various roles to facilitate junior faculty growth. Equally important, the chair should help the junior faculty member to set out a specific plan for development. Exhibits 8.1 and 8.2 list support mechanisms that the department chair can put into place so that the new faculty member can develop a realistic and comprehensive plan for development. The suggestions in Exhibit 8.1 pertain to tangible, material resources that are helpful in years one through five. The suggestions in Exhibit 8.2 pertain to collegial support needed at different points during the first five years.

With a grasp of junior faculty needs, a thoughtful choice of roles to facilitate faculty growth, and the development of support mechanisms to assist junior faculty in career planning, chairs can greatly facilitate the success of the newest members of their departments. If junior faculty perform well, chairs who have assisted them certainly will share in the credit and be applauded for their efforts.

Exhibit 8.1. Tangible Resources for Professional Support, Years One Through Five

Year One

1. Provide symbols of institutional identification or belonging. Items could be writing materials, briefcases, clothing, or pins with institutional logos and other identification.

2. Provide a list of community services and resources available. This list could include recreational, housing, and medical entries. Sometimes these lists are already available elsewhere (for example, the local Chamber of Commerce), but they can be tailored to the institution.

3. Provide start-up funds for laboratory and equipment, secretarial support, graduate research or teaching assistants, and computers, as needed.

4. Pay dues for the appropriate professional society for the first year. Some chairs take this action as a symbolic gesture of commitment to faculty development as well as in recognition that the process of becoming established the first year requires financial resources that some new faculty do not have.

5. Provide travel funds for professional society meetings. Once again, while the new faculty member is becoming established and finding out how to obtain resources, chairs often make support available, with the expectation that new faculty will progressively find more of their own resources.

6. Reduce teaching load or provide other load reduction to encourage good teaching as well as to establish a research program. Particularly for new faculty without previous teaching experience, chairs have found that overpreparation for classes can result in poor teaching as well as inadequate time devoted to research and writing.

Years Two Through Five

7. Encourage junior faculty to use internal and external resources to meet professional obligations. Chairs can nominate junior faculty for fellowships, society positions, and review panels to help them become known and better connected to resources.

8. Provide resources with an expectation that junior faculty members can find and parlay other resources over time to meet their goals. Often, a faculty member can consolidate diverse sources of modest funding into one complete, well-funded package.

Exhibit 8.2. Collegial Resources for Professional Support, Years One Through Five

Year One

1. Introduce the faculty member to campus leaders and resource people. Some faculty become isolated and unaware of resources available to improve their professional lives.

2. Provide an orientation to the institution and the department. This orientation is most effective when conducted as an ongoing process and not as a one-time activity.

3. Arrange or facilitate mentor relationships. Although all faculty may not desire mentors, these relationships have proved helpful to junior faculty success.

4. Periodically schedule sessions (over coffee or lunch breaks) to discuss concerns and answer "how to" questions. In addition to being useful to the junior faculty members, these sessions enable the chair to monitor progress and make appropriate interventions as needed.

5. Facilitate professional development plans for a period of two to five years. This planning helps to ensure that both short-term needs and long-term goals are addressed.

6. Ensure that professional progress is discussed beyond the annual evaluation conference. Feedback from the chair, the promotion and tenure committee, and senior faculty needs to be interpreted for the junior faculty member.

Years Two Through Five

7. Periodically schedule sessions to discuss concerns and to facilitate growth and development. Listen and ask "What do you want to do?" and "How can I help you do it?"

8. Invite junior faculty to participate in projects and proposals, whether the chair's own projects or those of the department.

9. Continue to encourage junior faculty to make appropriate time allotments for priority activities and to eliminate unnecessary commitments. They often need help in learning to say no and in preventing overcommitment.

10. Encourage participation in development activities both on and off campus to meet needs and to strengthen professional expertise and skills. Faculty often need guidance to address areas of professional performance that need to be strengthened. Chairs should have open and honest communications about strengthening areas of weakness or underdevelopment.

11. Provide evaluation and feedback on professional progress. Evaluative feedback helps to ensure that individuals are realistic about their roles and expectations and that they make the necessary adjustments for success.

References

Baldwin, R. G. "Faculty Career Stages and Implications for Professional Development." In J. H. Schuster, D. W. Wheeler, and Associates (eds.), *Enhancing Faculty Careers: Strategies for Development and Renewal.* San Francisco: Jossey-Bass, 1990.

Baldwin, R. G., and Blackburn, R. T. "The Academic Career as a Developmental Process: Implications for Higher Education." *Journal of Higher Education,* 1981, 52 (6), 598-614.

Boice, R. "New Faculty as Teachers." *Journal of Higher Education,* 1991, 62 (2), 150-173.

Bowen, H. R., and Schuster, J. H. *American Professors: A National Resource Imperiled.* New York: Oxford University, 1986.

Creswell, J. W., Wheeler, D. W., Seagren, A. T., Egly, N. J., and Beyer, K. D. *The Academic Chairperson's Handbook.* Lincoln: University of Nebraska Press, 1990.

Egly, N. J. "Academic Socialization and Faculty Development Assistance: A Study of New Tenure-Track Faculty Members in the Institute of Agriculture and Natural Resources." Unpublished doctoral dissertation, Department of Vocational and Adult Education, University of Nebraska, 1991.

Fink, L. D. (ed.). *The First Year of College Teaching.* New Directions for Teaching and Learning, no. 17. San Francisco: Jossey-Bass, 1984.

Lewis, K. G., and Povlacs, J. T. *Face to Face: A Sourcebook of Individual Consultation Techniques for Faculty/Instructional Developers.* Stillwater, Okla.: New Forums, 1988.

Lucas, A. F. (ed.). *The Department Chairperson's Role in Enhancing College Teaching.* New Directions for Teaching and Learning, no. 37. San Francisco: Jossey-Bass, 1989.

Lucas, A. F. "The Department Chair as Change Agent." In P. Seldin and Associates (eds.), *How Administrators Can Improve Teaching: Moving from Talk to Action in Higher Education.* San Francisco: Jossey-Bass, 1990.

McKeachie, W. J. *Teaching Tips: A Guidebook for the Beginning College Teacher.* Lexington, Mass.: Heath, 1986.

Mathis, B. C. "Academic Careers and Adult Development: A Nexus for Research." *Current Issues in Higher Education,* 1979, *2,* 21-24.

Menges, R. J. "Career-Span Faculty Development." *College Teaching,* 1985, *33,* 181-184.

Schuster, J. H., Wheeler, D. W., and Associates (eds.). *Enhancing Faculty Careers: Strategies for Development and Renewal.* San Francisco: Jossey-Bass, 1990.

Sorcinelli, M. D. "Chairs and the Development of New Faculty." *Department Advisor,* 1989, *5* (2), 1-4.

Sorcinelli, M. D., and Near, J. "Relationships Between Work and Life Away from Work Among University Faculty." *Journal of Higher Education,* 1989, *60* (1), 59-81.

Tucker, A. *Chairing the Academic Department.* New York: Macmillan, 1984.

Daniel W. Wheeler is coordinator of the Office of Professional and Organizational Development at the Institute of Agriculture and Natural Resources, University of Nebraska, Lincoln.

SUMMARY AND FURTHER REFLECTIONS

New and junior faculty are an exciting resource for colleges and universities; they are key contributors to the learning and lives of students and other faculty and to the quality of the institutional environment. Yet, as the chapter authors of this volume have argued, the evidence is strong that new faculty members experience significant and compelling challenges. The new and junior faculty as individuals and the colleges and universities in which they work benefit from thoughtful attention to strategies and approaches that help these novices develop as effective faculty members across the range of their responsibilities.

The research on new and junior faculty points to several themes weaving through their experience. We summarize here the research findings concerning each of these themes.

Need to Develop Teaching Skills. Research findings show that new and junior faculty find their teaching responsibilities overwhelming and stressful (Boice, 1991; Fink, 1984). Heavy teaching loads and the extensive preparation time required when one is developing courses are part of the story. The ways in which junior faculty approach their teaching, however, also contribute to the stress and overload. Boice (1991) has shown that new faculty, harboring concerns about student ratings, feel that they should emphasize course content and should lecture as a way to impart content. Although they want to teach well, they do not know how to go about improving and have little time to think about and reflect on their teaching. Most have not had any guidance or advice about using more creative teaching methods, such as those involving small group work, critical thinking, and active student involvement. Among those faculty who participate in faculty development activities, however, behaviors are different. They spend less time preparing to teach and more time doing scholarly writing, yet they feel more comfortable with their teaching. The message seems clear: Junior faculty need opportunities to learn about teaching.

Desire for Colleagueship. A great disappointment in the level of collegiality that they experience is one of the dominant themes in the research on new and junior faculty. These newer faculty members feel a sense of isolation and a need for supportive and stimulating interaction with other faculty (Boice, 1991; Whitt, 1991). Studying new faculty more than a decade ago, Fink (1984) reported that two-thirds of his respondents had very limited or no intellectual exchange with colleagues. Based on more recent research, Olsen and Sorcinelli (this volume) report that almost one-half of the junior faculty in their longitudinal study had expected their senior colleagues to extend more guidance and support. Over the five pretenure years, these junior faculty indicated that their satisfaction diminished in regard to the support and recognition for teaching and scholarship offered by their colleagues and administrators. Junior faculty want to experience the kind of collegiality that supports their professional growth, 'opens avenues for intellectual interchange, and provides feedback and recommendations. Typically, however, they feel alone and isolated as they face a panorama of new expectations.

Uncertainty About Institutional Expectations and Resources. Junior faculty members need the support that collegiality provides. But they also need information about the institution's expectations for their work and knowledge about the institutional resources available to assist them in their work. Often, though, junior faculty do not feel strong institutional support as they deal with pressures and challenges. In fact, in his study of first-year teachers, Fink (1984) found that their most frequently cited recommendation was that the university provide better information. The need for institutional attention to this problem of inadequate information and support is even more important in the face of expectations that junior faculty thrive quickly. Studying new faculty in a university's college of education, Whitt (1991) found that department chairs expect faculty to "hit the ground running." The challenge for new faculty is not only to survive in the early years but also to excel.

Stress from Multiple Demands. A frequent theme in the research findings concerning junior faculty and their work is that they put in long hours yet feel that demands exceed their time (Carnegie Foundation for the Advancement of Teaching, 1989; Finkelstein, 1984; Sorcinelli, 1988; Whitt, 1991). These demands also cause work time to spill over into leisure and family time (Sorcinelli and Near, 1989). Considerable stress results from the pressures of diverse responsibilities and the need to balance teaching, service, and research. Sorcinelli and Olsen (this volume) report that in their study of a cohort of faculty moving through the initial five years in their jobs, the proportion of those feeling very stressed increased considerably over time. Worry and stress over whether they can succeed in meeting and juggling multiple demands are consistent themes in the lives of junior faculty.

In this volume, we argue that new and junior faculty need not be left to struggle and muddle through these challenges on their own. We have presented a variety of formal and informal strategies, some involving minimal expense, that are effective in helping junior faculty carry out their various roles with success and confidence. The chapters suggest various models for orientation programs and areas that these programs might cover, strategies for stimulating effective mentoring relationships, and ideas for helping junior faculty "hit the ground running," (Whitt, 1991) in the research and teaching arenas.

Specific programs are not the only recommendations, however. We also argue that established faculty and institutional leaders—including department chairs, directors of faculty development or instructional improvement centers, and senior administrative leaders—can assist new faculty by modeling roles, providing timely and useful suggestions regarding available resources, and articulating the value of the institution's programs and efforts to support new faculty. Institutional leaders also can develop their own awareness of the issues confronting new faculty and can help their junior colleagues become involved in the informal campus networks that link faculty across departments.

Higher education is in an era of high levels of anticipated faculty retirements, an increasingly diverse student body, and serious fiscal constraints. The responsiveness of our colleges and universities to a wide array of societal expectations and demands depends on the creativity and effectiveness of each faculty member. Furthermore, in a time when the recruitment of excellent faculty is increasingly difficult, especially in some fields, universities and colleges are wise to put as much emphasis on integrating new faculty into their roles as on finding replacements for vacated positions. When a university or college helps junior faculty learn about their multiple roles and become confident members of the academic community, both the career experiences of the faculty and the quality of the institution are enriched.

Ann E. Austin
Mary Deane Sorcinelli
Editors

References

Boice, R. "New Faculty as Teachers." *Journal of Higher Education*, 1991, 62 (2), 150–173.

Carnegie Foundation for the Advancement of Teaching. *The Condition of the Professoriate: Attitudes and Trends, 1989*. Princeton, N.J.: Carnegie Foundation for the Advancement of Teaching, 1989.

Fink, L. D. (ed.). *The First Year of College Teaching*. New Directions for Teaching and Learning, no. 17. San Francisco: Jossey-Bass, 1984.

Finkelstein, M. J. *The American Academic Profession*. Columbus: Ohio State University Press, 1984.

Sorcinelli, M. D. "Satisfactions and Concerns of New University Teachers." *To Improve the Academy*, 1988, 7, 121–131.

Sorcinelli, M. D., and Near, J. "Relations Between Work and Life Away from Work Among University Faculty." *Journal of Higher Education*, 1989, 60 (1), 59–81.

Whitt, E. J. " 'Hit the Ground Running': Experiences of New Faculty in a School of Education." *Review of Higher Education*, 1991, 14 (2), 177–197.

ANN E. AUSTIN is associate professor in the Development of Educational Administration at Michigan State University, East Lansing.

MARY DEANE SORCINELLI is director of the Center for Teaching and associate adjunct professor in the Division of Educational Policy and Administration at the University of Massachusetts, Amherst.

INDEX

Ordering Information

New Directions for Teaching and Learning is a series of paperback books that presents ideas and techniques for improving college teaching, based both on the practical expertise of seasoned instructors and on the latest research findings of educational and psychological researchers. Books in the series are published quarterly in Fall, Winter, Spring, and Summer and are available for purchase by subscription as well as by single copy.

Subscriptions for 1992 cost $45.00 for individuals (a savings of 20 percent over single-copy prices) and $60.00 for institutions, agencies, and libraries. Please do not send institutional checks for personal subscriptions. Standing orders are accepted.

Single copies cost $14.95 when payment accompanies order. (California, New Jersey, New York, and Washington, D.C., residents please include appropriate sales tax.) Billed orders will be charged postage and handling.

Discounts for quantity orders are available. Please write to the address below for information.

All orders must include either the name of an individual or an official purchase order number. Please submit your order as follows:
Subscriptions: specify series and year subscription is to begin
Single copies: include individual title code (such as TL1)

Mail all orders to:
Jossey-Bass Publishers
350 Sansome Street
San Francisco, California 94104

For sales outside of the United States contact:
Maxwell Macmillan International Publishing Group
866 Third Avenue
New York, New York 10022